Inn Time
for
Breakfast
...Again

A Cookbook & Travel Guide
from Innkeepers of the Michigan
Lake to Lake Bed & Breakfast Association

Amherst Press
a division of Palmer Publications, Inc.
Amherst, Wisconsin

Copyright © 1997 Amherst Press

First Edition

ISBN 0-942495-60-8

Library of Congress Catalog Card Number: 96-079584

Published by
Amherst Press
A division of Palmer Publications, Inc.
PO Box 296
Amherst, Wisconsin 54406

Printed in the United States of America by
Palmer Publications, Inc.
318 North Main Street
Amherst, Wisconsin 54406

Designed and marketed by
Amherst Press

Contents

Acknowledgments

*Thank you to the cookbook committee of the Michigan
Lake to Lake Bed & Breakfast Association and
all the participating members.*

*Thank you to the creative staff at Amherst Press
and watercolor artist Kathleen Parr McKenna
for their contributions to the book's cover.*

Participating Inns

State Map
of Participating
Cities

•KEARSARGE

LAURIUM
•HOUGHTON

• BIG BAY

PETOSKEY
CHARLEVOIX

SUTTONS BAY • •CENTRAL LAKE •ATLANTA

•GRAYLING

TRAVERSE CITY

FRANKFORT•

EAST TAWAS•

•CADILLAC

LUDINGTON •

•PENTWATER

ST. LOUIS•
ALMA•

WHITEHALL• •FRANKENMUTH
MUSKEGON•
•FRUITPORT ITHACA• •CLIO
GRAND HAVEN• •SPRING LAKE

•IONIA

HOLLY•

•HOLLAND

DOUGLAS •SAUGATUCK
• •FENNVILLE
GLENN• •ALLEGAN CANTON•
ANN ARBOR• •YPSILANTI
•SOUTH HAVEN •GRASS LAKE
KALAMAZOO• •BROOKLYN
MARSHALL •JONESVILLE

•ST. JOSEPH

•COLDWATER

•UNION PIER

Guide by City of Participating Inns

Bed & Breakfast Profiles and Recipes

Castle in the Country
Bed & Breakfast

340 M-40 South
Allegan, MI 49010
616-673-8054

Hosts: Herb and Ruth Boven

*E*nchanting evenings begin at our 1906 Victorian castle. Luxurious original details inside the castle and charming country views encourage you to relax and experience the beautiful surroundings which will delight your senses and refresh your spirit.

We'll pamper you as our royal house guests with fresh flowers, candlelight, private dining, and hot cocoa at bedtime.

Minutes to fine dining, shopping, antiquing, art galleries, downhill and cross-country skiing, a nature and bicycling trail, canoeing, horseback riding, lakeshore activities, and small-town festivals. A delightful gourmet breakfast is served in your guest room or in our formal dining room.

Rates at Castle in the Country Bed & Breakfast range from $75-$145.
Rates include a full breakfast.

Cinnamon Sensation Coffee Cake

Our guests experience a "smell" sensation when this coffee cake is baking in the oven. Its rich brown topping and attractive swirl pattern make it a wonderful addition to any breakfast. Serve warm and wait for the compliments!

makes one 9x9-inch pan

1/4 cup (1/2 stick) margarine, softened

3/4 cup sugar

1 egg, slightly beaten

1 1/2 cups flour

2 teaspoons baking powder

1/2 teaspoon salt

1 cup milk

1 teaspoon vanilla extract

Topping:

1 cup brown sugar

3 tablespoons flour

2 teaspoons cinnamon

4 tablespoons margarine

1/2 cup walnuts or pecans, finely chopped

Preheat oven to 350 degrees. Spray a 9x9-inch pan with nonstick cooking spray.

In a medium bowl, cream margarine and sugar; beat in egg. Sift together flour, baking powder, and salt in a separate bowl. Add to creamed mixture alternately with milk. Stir in vanilla. Pour mixture into prepared pan.

To make topping, in a small bowl, mix together sugar, flour, and cinnamon. Cut in margarine with pastry blender or fork. Spoon half of topping over batter. Using a knife, make swirls through mixture. Spoon remaining topping over batter and sprinkle with nuts.

Bake 30 minutes, or until wooden pick inserted in center comes out clean. Serve warm.

Saravilla Bed & Breakfast

633 North State Street
Alma, MI 48801
517-463-4078

Hosts: Linda and Jon Darrow

Saravilla, easily accessible from anywhere in the lower peninsula, is an 11,000-square-foot Dutch Colonial home built in 1894 as a summer "cottage." Listed on the Michigan Historical Register, it is truly a delight to appreciate the imported woods, magnificent craftsmanship, original wall coverings, light fixtures, leaded glass windows, and built-ins.

The six quiet and spacious guest rooms (three with fireplaces) have private baths and are individually decorated. Play a game of pool in the billiard room or soak in the hot tub in our sun room.

Beverages and snacks are always available, and a full breakfast is served in our elegant turret dining room.

Rates at Saravilla Bed & Breakfast range from $55-$85.
Rates include a full breakfast.

Friendship Granola

Looking for something different to serve at breakfast or as a snack? This recipe makes a large quantity and keeps well. It makes a perfect Christmas gift when packaged in decorative containers. The recipe comes from a Mennonite community which emphasizes eating better and consuming less in a world with limited resources. If ingredients are purchased in bulk, there is an even greater savings over commercial "natural" cereals.

makes 20 cups

1/2 cup oil	1/2 cup sesame seeds
1 cup (2 sticks) margarine	1 cup chopped nuts
2 tablespoons molasses	2 cups Grape Nuts cereal
1 tablespoon vanilla extract	1 cup wheat germ
1 cup brown sugar	1 pound coconut flakes
1 cup honey	1 cup sunflower seeds
1/2 teaspoon salt	1 cup raisins (optional)
2 pounds regular rolled oats	

In a large bowl, microwave oil, margarine, molasses, vanilla, sugar, honey, and salt until melted. Let cool slightly; add oats, sesame seeds, nuts, cereal, wheat germ, coconut flakes, and sunflower seeds. Stir thoroughly. Spread in 3 ungreased 15 1/2 x 10 1/2-inch pans.

Bake in a 350-degree oven 20-25 minutes, stirring every 5-7 minutes. Remove from oven to cool; add raisins. Store in a 5-quart airtight container.

The Urban Retreat

2759 Canterbury Road
Ann Arbor, MI 48104
313-971-8110

Hosts: Gloria Krys and André Rosalik

This contemporary ranch homestay has provided quiet comfort to business and pleasure travelers since 1986.

Minutes from downtown Ann Arbor, The Urban Retreat is tucked away on a tree-lined street; the adjacent parkland offers miles of walking trails. Guest rooms and common areas are lovingly furnished with antiques. The Retreat is air-conditioned and is home to several friendly house cats. Gourmet breakfasts are served overlooking the gardens.

The Urban Retreat is a member of the National Wildlife Federation's "Backyard Wildlife Habitat Program." We welcome guests from all cultures, races, and lifestyles.

Rates at The Urban Retreat range from $55-$65.
Rates include a full breakfast.

Pear-Sausage Soufflé

Crisp fall mornings call for hearty breakfasts, and this dish fits the bill elegantly. Partial preparation the night before also allows for a few extra winks of sleep.

serves 4

1 tablespoon butter, room
   temperature
4 slices firm white bread
   (Pepperidge Farm works well)
4 large eggs, beaten
1 cup evaporated milk
1¹/₂ teaspoons sugar
¹/₈ teaspoon freshly ground nutmeg

2 ripe pears, pared, cored
   and sliced
   Fresh lemon juice
4 ounces bulk sausage,
   cooked and drained
¹/₄ cup shredded Cheddar
   cheese

Spray 4 individual au gratin or casserole dishes with nonstick cooking spray.

Lightly spread butter on bread. Place butter side down in each dish.

Combine eggs, milk, sugar, and nutmeg in a medium bowl. Pour mixture over bread slices, dividing evenly among dishes. Cover with plastic wrap and refrigerate overnight.

Dip pear slices in lemon juice. Layer sausage, then pear slices over bread. Bake at 325 degrees for 25 minutes. Sprinkle with cheese; bake 5 minutes longer or until cheese melts. Serve hot.

The Briley Inn

11021 McArthur Road
Atlanta, MI 49709
517-785-4784

Hosts: William and Carla Gardner

This elegant redwood Inn, decorated in antique Victorian, has impressive windows overlooking Thunder Bay River. The Inn features a great room and cozy den with fireplace, just perfect when afternoon tea is served. A Jacuzzi, central air-conditioning, and cable TV round out the amenities. Canoes and boats can be rented and golf packages on nearby courses are also available. The Inn is located in the heart of northern Michigan's elk country with hiking, fishing, skiing, and snow-mobiling all nearby and is closed during the month of November.

Rates at The Briley Inn range from $50-$65.
Rates include a full country breakfast.

Ginger Pancakes with Fresh Peach Topping

This recipe was given to us by a foreign guest and is served on a regular basis at the Inn. Because our guests enjoy it so much, we often are asked to share the recipe with them. Don't wait for breakfast to serve this; try it for brunch or even as a luncheon item. It's good anytime.

serves 4-6

1 cup flour
1/2 teaspoon baking soda
1/2 teaspoon salt
1/2 teaspoon ground ginger
1/2 teaspoon cinnamon
1/8 teaspoon ground cloves
6 tablespoons molasses
2 large eggs
1 cup sour cream or buttermilk
2 tablespoons butter, melted

Topping:
1/2 cup (1 stick) butter or margarine, melted
3/4 cup maple syrup, or 1 cup brown sugar
3-4 cups fresh or frozen sliced peaches
Dash of cinnamon (optional)

Combine flour, baking soda, salt, ginger, cinnamon, and cloves in a medium bowl.

In a small bowl, whisk together molasses, eggs, and sour cream; add butter. Add to flour mixture, stirring until just combined.

To make topping, in a medium saucepan, combine butter and syrup. Simmer 5 minutes. Add peaches; simmer covered 5 minutes longer, or until fresh peaches are tender. Add cinnamon; keep warm.

Heat griddle over moderate heat until drops of water scatter over surface. Brush with cooking oil or butter. Drop batter by 1/4 cupfuls onto griddle. Cook until air bubbles form over entire surface. Turn and cook other side.

Serve with peach topping and a dollop of whipped cream, if desired.

Big Bay Point Lighthouse
Bed & Breakfast

3 Lighthouse Road
PO Box 3
Big Bay, MI 49808
906-345-9957

Hosts: Linda and Jeff Gamble

*H*igh atop a cliff jutting into the waters of Lake Superior, the lighthouse beckons to travelers in search of a secluded retreat from modern life—a unique bed and breakfast in one of the few surviving resident working lighthouses in the country.

The seven guest rooms, all with private baths, have views of the lake or the hardwood and pine forest. Early risers can be rewarded with sunrises and views of deer and fox. Stories of lighthouse history and storms at sea accompany the lighthouse keeper's full breakfast.

Boat, bike, ski and snowshoe rentals, fishing supplies, and wilderness guides are all available locally. Antique shops, museums, festivals, and winter sports competitions are only a short drive away.

Rates at Big Bay Point Lighthouse Bed & Breakfast range from $85-$155.
Rates include a full breakfast.

Cheese Blintzes

Cheese Blintzes are always a hit with our guests. We serve them with sour cream and fresh strawberries from the garden when in season. Blintzes are also good with blueberries and a sprinkling of confectioners' sugar.

makes 4 blintzes

Crepes:
- 1/2 cup flour
- 1 tablespoon sugar
- 1/2 teaspoon baking powder
- Pinch of salt
- 1 large egg
- 1/2 cup milk
- 1 tablespoon unsalted butter

Filling:
- 1 cup cottage cheese
- 1/4 cup grated farmer's cheese
- 2 tablespoons sugar
- 1/2 teaspoon lemon zest
- 1/2 teaspoon orange zest
- 1/2 teaspoon pure vanilla extract
- 1 egg yolk
- 2 tablespoons unsalted butter
- Confectioners' sugar (optional)

Stir together flour, sugar, baking powder, and salt in a medium bowl. In a separate bowl, stir together egg and milk. With a fork, quickly mix egg mixture into dry ingredients. Melt butter in a 5-inch crepe pan; add to batter; stir to mix. Place butter-coated pan over moderate heat. Ladle in only enough batter to cover the bottom, swirling to coat pan evenly. Cook just until edges turn golden. Remove with spatula and flip, cooked-side up, onto kitchen towel, folding ends of towel over crepe. Repeat process with remaining batter, stacking crepes inside towel.

Stir together cottage cheese and farmer's cheese, sugar, zests, vanilla, and egg yolk in a medium bowl. Place crepe, cooked-side up, on work surface. Spoon about 1 tablespoon of filling along center of crepe. Fold opposite ends in, then sides to enclose filling. Repeat with remaining crepes and filling.

Melt 2 tablespoons butter over moderate heat in a skillet large enough to hold all the blintzes without crowding. When skillet sizzles, add blintzes, seam side down, and fry until golden brown, 3-4 minutes per side. If desired, sprinkle with confectioners' sugar before serving.

The Chicago Street Inn

219 Chicago Street
PO Box 546
Brooklyn, MI 49230
517-592-3888

Hosts: Karen and Bill Kerr

The Chicago Street Inn is an 1886 Queen Anne Victorian house located in the heart of the Irish Hills in a picturesque Victorian village. The Inn is appointed with family and area antiques and is set against a background of marvelous original oak and cherry woodwork. The Victorian house has two quaint rooms with private baths and two Victorian Jacuzzi suites—one with a fireplace.

The 1920s bungalow has two Jacuzzi suites with fireplaces. Both houses are smoke-free and have central air-conditioning. This is an area of antiquing, hiking, biking, parks, great food, and relaxation.

Rates at The Chicago Street Inn range from $80-$165.
Rates include a full breakfast.

Potato Delight

This recipe was given to us by a pair of 78-year-old twins. A versatile and delicious recipe which can be served hot from the oven, at room temperature, or re-heated the next day. We like to serve it with omelettes. It's great to take to potluck suppers and can also be featured as a main dish. Plan to make it the night before, refrigerating until baking.

serves 10

  10 large potatoes
    6 slices lean bacon, uncooked, diced
1^1/$_2$ cups diced onion
 1/4 pound Velveeta cheese, diced
 1/4 cup chopped green olives
    1 cup mayonnaise

Peel and quarter potatoes. In a large kettle, cover with water and cook until fork-tender, but firm. Cool; dice and place in a large bowl. Add bacon, onions, cheese, olives, and mayonnaise; mix until well blended. Place in a 13x9-inch baking dish; cover and refrigerate overnight.

Preheat oven to 350 degrees.

Remove pan from refrigerator, uncover, and bring ingredients to room temperature. Bake for 1 hour, or until top is brown and cheese is bubbling.

Dewey Lake Manor
Bed & Breakfast

11811 Laird Road
Brooklyn, MI 49230
517-467-7122

Hosts: Joe and Barbara Phillips

Sitting atop a knoll overlooking Dewey Lake, a "country retreat" awaits Manor guests in the Irish Hills of southern Michigan. This Italianate-style house was built in the late 1860s by A. F. Dewey, one of five brothers whose father came "west" as a surveyor. A. F. Dewey was "a prosperous farmer of the area," owning much land including the lake.

This century-old home, furnished with antiques and original kerosene chandeliers, has five bedrooms with private baths and two bedrooms with fireplaces and central air. Guests may enjoy the paddleboat and canoe or picnics and bonfires by the lake. Golf and antiquing are nearby.

Rates at Dewey Lake Manor Bed & Breakfast range from $55-$75.
Rates include a full breakfast.

Waffles by Joe

This recipe was developed out of desperation. I am no "cook" but love waffles, and the box recipes just didn't "have it." This is quick, easy, and delicious and has become a favorite with our guests. I use a Belgian waffle iron for decorative waffle shapes. Serve with fresh butter and pure Michigan maple syrup.

makes 4 waffles

1 large egg
1 cup buttermilk
$1/2$ cup pecan pancake mix
$1/2$ cup buckwheat pancake mix
1 tablespoon vegetable oil
$1/8$ teaspoon baking powder

In a medium bowl, beat egg well with wire whisk. Add buttermilk to blend. Gradually add pecan and buckwheat pancake mixes to egg mixture, whisking constantly. Add oil and baking powder; mix until well blended.

Pour batter onto hot waffle iron (approximately $1/2$ cup batter per waffle). Close cover and bake 4 minutes. Gently lift waffle from iron with fork and serve immediately.

Hoxeyville Hills
Bed & Breakfast

7143 West 48 Road-Hoxeyville
Cadillac, MI 49601
616-862-3628

Hosts: Patricia Gutierrez and Pierre Tretter

*H*oxeyville Hills is a country retreat nestled in the Manistee National Forest. Our hilltop home overlooks 90 acres of trees, ridges, meadows, a pond, and barn. Deer, wild turkey, birds, and other animals abound in our certified wildlife habitat.

Our property and the forest trails and lakes are ideal for winter and summer activities. Caberfae Peaks Resort and the Pine River are minutes away. Drive to the nearby towns of Cadillac and Manistee, or just relax and bask in our beautiful surroundings.

Our private luxurious four-room suite includes a screen porch, deck, gazebo, fireplace, Jacuzzi, pool table, and cable TV. Guests will enjoy a hearty gourmet breakfast, evening dessert tray, snacks, and warm hospitality.

Rates at Hoxeyville Hills Bed & Breakfast range from $125-$145.
Rates include a full breakfast.

Sausage and Apple Quiche

This recipe can be partially prepared the night before and refrigerated until eggs are added and quiche is baked. I like to serve it on chilly mornings accompanied by baked spiced fruit and homemade maple scones.

makes one 9-inch quiche

1   pastry shell, 9 inches
1/2   pound bulk spicy sausage
1/2   cup chopped onion
3/4   cup peeled, shredded tart
    apple
1   tablespoon lemon juice
1   tablespoon sugar
1/8   teaspoon crushed red
    pepper flakes

1   cup shredded Cheddar
    cheese
3   eggs
1 1/2   cups half-and-half
1/4   teaspoon salt
    Dash of ground black pepper

Bake pastry shell according to recipe or package instructions or until lightly browned. Remove from oven to cool; set aside.

Crumble sausage into a large skillet. Add onion and cook over medium heat until meat is browned and onion is tender; drain well.

Return pan to heat and add apple, lemon juice, sugar, and pepper flakes. Cook over medium-high heat, stirring constantly, or until apple is just tender and all liquid is evaporated, about 4 minutes. Remove from heat to cool. Spoon sausage mixture into baked shell and top with cheese. Recipe can be held overnight at this point by covering and placing in refrigerator.

Preheat oven to 375 degrees.

In a medium bowl, whisk together eggs, half-and-half, salt, and pepper. Pour over sausage mixture. Bake 35-45 minutes, or until knife inserted in center comes out clean. Let stand 10 minutes before serving.

Willow Brook Inn
Bed & Breakfast

44255 Warren Road
Canton, MI 48187
313-454-0019 or 888-454-1919

Hosts: Bernadette and Michael Van Lenten

Childhood memories…simple pleasures. Willow Brook winds its way through the backyard of this Inn, situated on a wooded acre. The four guest rooms are filled with country antiques and feather beds with down comforters. A whirlpool bath and special keepsakes from childhood add a unique touch.

Your candlelight breakfast consists of delicacies such as seasonal fresh fruit, scones topped with Devon cream, a rich egg dish, and pancakes or stuffed French toast.

Area attractions include Greenfield Village; the Detroit Zoo; Pheasant Run Golf Course; The Summit and local antique and gift shops. The Inn is ten miles from Metro Airport and two miles from I-275. Special packages are also available.

Rates at Willow Brook Inn Bed & Breakfast range from $75-$105.
Rates include a full breakfast.

Harvest Pancakes

Although our guests request these pancakes all year-round, fall is a perfect time to serve them. Ingredients such as wheat flour and buttermilk, along with tart apples and pecans, provide a healthy breakfast entree.

makes 8-12 pancakes

1 cup flour	1¹/2 cups buttermilk
1 cup wheat flour	1/2 teaspoon baking soda
1/2 teaspoon salt	1 egg, well beaten
3/4 teaspoon baking powder	1 tablespoon butter, melted
1 tablespoon sugar	1 cup grated tart apple
1/2 teaspoon cinnamon	1/2 cup chopped pecans

Mix together flours, salt, baking powder, sugar, and cinnamon in a large bowl; stir to blend.

Combine buttermilk with baking soda in a medium bowl; add egg and butter; mix well. Add to flour mixture; stir quickly to blend. Fold apple and pecans into mixture.

Pour pancakes, approximately 3 inches in size, on greased hot griddle and fry until brown on both sides.

Serve with warm maple syrup.

Bridgewalk Bed & Breakfast

2287 South Main Street
PO Box 399
Central Lake, MI 49622
616-544-8122

Hosts: Janet and Tom Meteer

A footbridge is the first step to the special charm of Bridgewalk, leading you across a meandering brook to the front porch. There you can enjoy the porch swing or relax on the deck to the sounds of the brook. Built in 1895, our spacious country-Victorian has five guest bedrooms, each decorated with antiques and quilts, all with private baths.

Breakfast, served in the dining room or on the deck, is a delightful way to begin a day of boating, biking, golfing, antiquing, or enjoying the areas of Torch Lake, Lake Michigan, Grass River Natural Area, or the Jordon River Pathway.

Rates at Bridgewalk Bed & Breakfast range from $75-$85.
Rates include a full breakfast.

Apple Sausage Blossoms

These "blossoms" are a wonderful make-ahead breakfast entree. Prepare fill-ing the night before and assemble and bake the next morning. Serve with chilled fruit soup and scones for a perfect accompaniment.

makes 8 blossoms

2 eggs, divided
1 pound pork sausage,
     uncooked
1 onion, minced (approxi-
     mately 1/2 to 3/4 cup)
3 apples, peeled and
     chopped
3/4 cup bread cubes

1/2 teaspoon cinnamon
1 teaspoon sage
2 tablespoons brown sugar
1 sheet frozen puff pastry,*
     thawed
   Apples and sage leaves for
     garnish

Preheat oven to 400 degrees.

Beat 1 of the eggs in a large bowl. Add sausage, onion, and apples. Combine bread cubes, cinnamon, sage, and brown sugar in a small bowl. Sprinkle over sausage mixture and combine until evenly distributed.

On floured surface, cut pastry into 8 equal sections. Using a rolling pin, roll each section into a 5- to 6-inch square. Place 1/8 of sausage mixture onto middle of pastry square. Gather corners of pastry square above sausage mix-ture, grasp near filling, and twist to seal. Separate points to resemble a blos-som. Repeat process until all blossoms have been assembled. Beat remaining egg and brush over blossom. Place on cookie sheet and bake 35-40 minutes until browned. Serve immediately.

*Note: A 171/4-ounce package contains 2 sheets of puff pastry. Keep remaining sheet frozen for later use.

Coulter Creek
Bed & Breakfast

7900 Darmon Place
PO Box 427
Central Lake, MI 49622
616-544-3931 or 800-942-6858

Hostess: Joyce Slater

*E*njoy the gently revitalizing "country yard" setting with panoramic views of beautiful Hanley Lake, a private beach, dock, gardens, and hot tub.

Our 1890s colonial-style home is extremely comfortable, with tastefully decorated rooms and guest-pleasing breakfasts. The towns of Charlevoix, Bellaire, Alden, Elk Rapids, and Traverse City are a beautiful country drive away. There's skiing, golf, unique shopping, and fine dining including Tapawingo and the Rowe Inn—two of the top-rated gourmet restaurants in Michigan. We are confident that once you visit our bed and breakfast and surrounding area, it will become a favorite getaway.

Rates at Coulter Creek Bed & Breakfast range from $60-$85.
Rates include a full breakfast.

Make Ahead Eggs Benedict

Prepared the evening before, this recipe makes a wonderful entree, taking only a few minutes of your valuable morning time. For a spicier variation, substitute Monterey Jack Hot Pepper cheese for the Swiss cheese. Low-fat milk may be substituted for whole milk.

serves 8

4 white or whole grain English
   muffins, split and toasted
8 slices (2 ounces each)
   turkey-ham
8 eggs, divided

1 teaspoon paprika
1/8 teaspoon ground nutmeg
1/8 teaspoon black pepper
2 cups milk
2 cups shredded Swiss cheese
1/4 cup white cooking wine

Sauce:
1/4 cup (1/2 stick) margarine,
   melted
1/4 cup flour

Topping:
1/2 cup crushed cornflakes
1 tablespoon margarine, melted

Arrange muffin halves in a 13x9-inch baking pan. Place 1 slice of turkey-ham on each half.

Fill a 12-inch skillet half full of water and bring to a boil. Break 4 of the eggs into boiling water; poach 3 minutes or until whites of egg are set. Remove eggs with a slotted spoon; place 1 egg on each muffin. Repeat process until all eggs are cooked.

To make sauce, melt margarine in a 2-quart saucepan. Stir in flour, paprika, nutmeg, and pepper. Add milk all at once; stir continuously and cook over medium heat until thickened, about 3-5 minutes. Add cheese and stir until melted, about 1 minute. Add wine; stir with wooden spoon until mixture is well blended, about 2 minutes. Spoon sauce over muffins.

To make topping, combine cornflakes and margarine in a small bowl; sprinkle over muffins. Cover pan and refrigerate overnight. Bake uncovered in a 350-degree oven for 20-25 minutes.

Belvedere Inn

306 Belvedere Avenue
Charlevoix, MI 49720
616-547-2251 or 800-280-4667

Hosts: Tim and Karen Watters

The Belvedere Inn was built in 1887 on Belvedere Avenue, just two blocks from downtown. This Inn and tree-lined street are near shopping, wonderful restaurants, marinas, golfing, and beaches. The antique-filled home has a wraparound porch and hammocks under 100-year-old trees. Either place is a perfect spot to relax. Each of the seven rooms are individually decorated and have their own private baths. Enjoy a full breakfast and evening dessert. You'll never be hungry!

Rates at Belvedere Inn range from $90-$120.
Rates include a full breakfast.

Buttermilk Cinnamon Bread

*When you bake this bread your whole house fills with a wonderful smell.
Your guests will enjoy the aroma of cinnamon as they awaken and
will love the flavor of this fresh, warm bread. If there are any leftovers,
try it toasted.*

makes 2 loaves

1/2 cup oil	4 cups flour
2 cups sugar	1/2 cup sugar
2 eggs	2 tablespoons cinnamon
2 cups buttermilk	1/2 teaspoon salt
2 teaspoons baking soda	

Preheat oven to 350 degrees. Spray two 9x5-inch loaf pans with nonstick cooking spray.

Mix together oil, sugar, eggs, buttermilk, baking soda, and flour in a large bowl. Pour 1 cup of the batter into each prepared pan.

Combine sugar, cinnamon, and salt in a small bowl. Sprinkle half of the sugar mixture over each pan; pour remaining batter equally between pans. Sprinkle remaining sugar mixture over batter. Using a knife, swirl through batter. Bake approximately 1 hour, or until wooden pick inserted in center comes out clean. Cool 10 minutes, then remove from pans and place on wire rack. Slice bread when completely cool.

Caine Cottage

219 Antrim
Charlevoix, MI 49720
616-547-6781

Hostess: Kendra Behrendt

Caine Cottage was built in circa 1891 and established as an Inn in 1992. It is located on a quiet residential street, just two blocks from Main Street and three blocks from Michigan Beach. There is a lovely front porch with wicker furniture for guests to enjoy in warm weather and a comfortable indoor sitting room for cooler days.

Caine Cottage is open year-round. There are many activities available in or near Charlevoix: golfing, boating, swimming, biking, hiking, and skiing, to name a few.

Rates at Caine Cottage range from $45-$125.
Rates include a full breakfast.

Pineapple Breakfast Bread

This easy-to-make quick bread is topped with brown sugar and pecans and covered by a rich orange glaze. The recipe makes two large loaves; enjoy one right from the oven and freeze one for unexpected guests. Also great for gift giving when baked in four small loaf pans. Wrap each loaf tightly with plastic wrap and add a decorative bow.

makes 2 large loaves or 4 small loaves

Bread:
- 2 eggs
- 1 1/2 cups sugar
- 1 can (15 ounces) crushed pineapple with juice
- 2 cups flour
- 1 teaspoon baking soda
- 1 teaspoon salt

Topping:
- 1/2 cup brown sugar
- 1/2 cup finely chopped pecans

Glaze:
- 1/2 cup (1 stick) margarine
- 1 can (5 ounces) evaporated milk
- 1 teaspoon orange extract

Preheat oven to 350 degrees or 325 degrees for nonstick pans.

To make bread, beat eggs in a large bowl. Add sugar, pineapple and juice; beat until well blended. Add flour, baking soda, and salt; beat until mixture is just blended. Do not overmix.

Pour mixture into two 9x5-inch or four 6x4-inch greased loaf pans.

To make topping, in a small bowl, combine sugar and pecans. Sprinkle topping evenly over each loaf. Bake 30-35 minutes, or until wooden pick inserted in center comes out clean.

To make glaze, combine margarine, evaporated milk, and orange extract in a small saucepan. Bring to a boil while stirring; remove from heat and set aside. Pour over loaves immediately after removing bread from oven.

Cool bread 10 minutes; remove from pans. When thoroughly cooled, store bread in airtight containers until ready to slice.

The Cinnamon Stick Farm
Bed and Breakfast

12364 North Genesee Road
Clio, MI 48420
810-686-8391

Hosts: Brian and Carol Powell

The Cinnamon Stick Bed & Breakfast is a unique country farm home which is set on 50 rolling acres in rural Genesee County. There are walking trails, a fishing pond, and a tennis court.

Quaint guest rooms reflect charming country antiques and comfortable beds. There is a large great room with a fieldstone fireplace and over-stuffed furniture and a dining room and living room for guests to enjoy. We serve a full country breakfast.

Minutes from the Clio Amphitheater, Crossroads Village, Frankenmuth, Birch Run Outlet Mall, Flint, Saginaw, and historic Chesaning, Cinnamon Stick Farm Bed and Breakfast is located just eight miles east of I-75, Clio exit #131 and is the hub of fun and relaxation.

Rates at The Cinnamon Stick Farm Bed & Breakfast range from $60-$75.
Rates include a full breakfast.

Country-Style Potato and Onion Pie

This egg and Swiss cheese quiche-like pie is a satisfying food that brings warmth to our breakfast table. If you have basil in your garden, substitute it for the parsley to give it that fresh-from-the-garden flavor.

serves 4

2 tablespoons butter or margarine
1 cup sliced new red potatoes
   ($1/8$-inch thick)
1 medium onion, sliced $1/8$-inch
   thick, separated into rings
$1 1/4$ cups shredded Swiss cheese
$1/3$ cup chopped fresh parsley or basil

$1/3$ cup milk
8 eggs, slightly beaten
$1/2$ teaspoon salt
$1/4$ teaspoon black pepper
1 medium ripe tomato,
   sliced $1/2$-inch thick

Preheat oven to 400 degrees.

Place butter in a medium ovenproof skillet and melt in oven. Add potatoes and onion. Bake, stirring once, until vegetables are crisp-tender, about 15-20 minutes.

In a large bowl, stir together cheese, parsley, milk, eggs, salt, and pepper. Pour over baked potatoes and onion; arrange tomato slices over eggs. Return to oven; continue baking an additional 20 minutes, or until eggs are set and lightly browned.

Chicago Pike Inn

215 East Chicago Street
Coldwater, MI 49036
517-279-8744

Hostess: Rebecca Schultz

This colonial reform mansion, built in 1903, has been renovated to its grand Victorian splendor. Eight beautifully restored rooms are individually decorated for pleasure and comfort and have many thoughtful touches. Innkeeper Becky and her staff have a knack for making your stay memorable with special little touches, like the 7:30 a.m. coffee provided for those early risers. This is followed by a scrumptious three-course breakfast served in the Inn's formal dining room. The library is a guest favorite and has a variety of books and magazines along with a three-tier candy table filled with delicious sweets. The Inn has many special amenities of luxury and grace for every special visitor. Please come and experience the splendor of the Chicago Pike Inn.

Rates at Chicago Pike Inn range from $80-$165.
Rates include a full breakfast.

Curried Fruit Bake

Here's a recipe that is simple to assemble, bake, and serve; yet it looks and tastes like you've really fussed! Make this ahead of time if you have a busy schedule—just pop it back in the oven until it begins to bubble. Serve this casserole dish for breakfast, as a side dish for lunch, or as a dessert to an evening meal.

makes one 13x9-inch pan

1 can (16 ounces) pineapple
   chunks, drained
1 can (16 ounces) sliced
   peaches, drained and cubed
1 can (16 ounces) sliced pears,
   drained and cubed
1 can (16 ounces) mandarin
   oranges, drained

1 jar (10 ounces) spiced apple
   rings, drained and cubed
1/2 cup (1 stick) butter or
   margarine
1 tablespoon cornstarch
1 teaspoon curry powder
3/4 cup brown sugar

Preheat oven to 350 degrees.

Butter a 13x9-inch casserole dish. In a large bowl, mix together pineapple, peaches, pears, mandarin oranges, and apple rings. Pour into prepared dish.

Melt butter in a small saucepan. Add cornstarch, curry powder, and brown sugar; stir until sugar is dissolved and mixture begins to thicken. Pour over fruit and stir carefully until well coated. Bake uncovered for 30 minutes. Remove from oven and serve in sherbet dishes while still hot.

The Kirby House

294 West Center Street
Douglas, MI 49406
616-857-2904

Hosts: Marsha and Loren Kontio

*T*he Kirby House sits as a resplendent example of the imagination of Sarah Kirby and the early 1890s. Sarah built her home in the Queen-Anne style with a wraparound porch, four fireplaces (two of which are in guest rooms), and five generous-size bedrooms. There are oak cupboards in the butler's pantry, a breakfront in the dining room, and leaded and prism glass windows. The home is furnished throughout with period antiques supplied by the owners' grandparents. The Innkeepers will gladly share stories of the home's rich history when it served as the local hospital, junk store, antique shop, local humane society, and real estate agency.

Through all the changes, the home's elegance remains intact with guests welcomed in the same tradition set by Sarah many years ago.

Rates at The Kirby House range from $75-$125.
Rates include a full breakfast.

Shaker Cheese Squares

Our guests love this recipe and we do too! Just mix together according to instructions; cover, refrigerate, and bake it in the morning. Save any leftovers for a lunchtime treat.

serves 8-10

8 eggs
1 carton (16 ounces) cottage cheese
1 pound American cheese, cut into chunks
1/2 cup (1 stick) butter, cut into chunks

6 tablespoons flour
1 package (10 ounces) frozen chopped spinach, thawed and well drained
1 tablespoon baking powder

Preheat oven to 350 degrees. Spray a 13x9-inch pan with nonstick cooking spray.

Beat eggs in a medium bowl. Add cottage cheese, American cheese, butter, flour, spinach, and baking powder; mix until well blended.

Pour into prepared pan and bake 45 minutes, or until top is golden brown. Let stand 10 minutes before cutting into squares and serving.

East Tawas Junction
Bed & Breakfast

514 West Bay Street
East Tawas, MI 48730
517-362-8006

Hosts: Leigh and Don Mott

*E*ast Tawas Junction Bed & Breakfast, a turn-of-the-century country Victorian home decorated in warmth and comfort, sets proudly on an estate-sized, tree-shaded lot overlooking Tawas Bay. Recent renovation provides five richly furnished bedrooms with private baths and TVs.

The comfortable parlor, glass-enclosed wraparound porch, and outdoor decks invite relaxation and fellowship. Biking, jogging, or romantic strolls along the blacktop path outlining Tawas Bay lead to the beautiful pier and boat docking facility, Tawas Bay Refuge Harbor, or to sandy beaches, shops, and restaurants. Golf courses are within a short drive. A full breakfast in the informal dining room is always a "special event" graciously served and setting the tone for congeniality, relaxation, and renewal.

Rates at East Tawas Junction Bed & Breakfast range from $59-$89.
Rates include a full breakfast.

Eggs en Cocotte Lorraine

This recipe is a delightful surprise as elegant as Eggs Benedict with a touch of flair. Wonderful served with pineapple fruit compote and yeast-risen corn bread with "jalapeno" strawberry jam! Decidedly a treat! Bacon may be substituted for the ham and half-and-half can replace the heavy cream.

serves 6

6 pieces thinly sliced Swiss
    cheese, cut in 1/2-inch strips
6 large eggs
6 pieces thinly sliced ham,
    chopped
   Salt and pepper

2/3 cup heavy cream
1/4 cup grated romano or
    Parmesan cheese
   Paprika
6 small sprigs parsley

Preheat oven to 450 degrees.

Place large pan of hot water in oven.

Spray 6 individual ramekins or souffle baking dishes with nonstick cooking spray. Place strips from each cheese slice in prepared dishes. Break an egg into each dish and puncture whites in several places with a knife, being careful to leave yolk intact. Sprinkle chopped ham on top of egg. Pour 2 tablespoons cream over ham. Sprinkle with romano cheese and season with salt and pepper, as desired.

Place in oven in pan so that hot water comes halfway up sides of dishes. Reduce temperature to 350 degrees; bake 20 minutes. Serve immediately, garnished with parsley sprigs.

The Kingsley House
Bed & Breakfast

626 West Main Street
Fennville, MI 49408
616-561-6425

Hosts: Gary and Kari King

"*E*legantly Victorian" best describes this Queen Anne-style tur-reted mansion. Built in 1886 and restored in 1990, The Kingsley House boasts eight guest rooms, each with a private bath and some with Jacuzzis and fireplaces. All of the rooms are named after apples in honor of the home's builder, Harvey Kingsley, who introduced apple trees to this area over 100 years ago.

The Inn is located just minutes from Saugatuck, Holland, and Lake Michigan beaches. In summer enjoy golfing, shopping, and water sports of all kinds. In winter we are just steps from cross-country ski-ing and ice skating. Bicycles are also available. Come relax with us!

Rates at The Kingsley House Bed & Breakfast range from $80-$145.
Rates include a full breakfast on weekends and a deluxe
continental breakfast during the week.

Honey-Glazed Pecan French Toast

This easy French toast is made the night before and baked in the morning. Our guests tell us that it is the best they have ever tasted! What a thrill to please guests with a recipe that is so quick and easy for us to prepare!

serves 8-10

1 loaf French bread	*Topping:*
3 large eggs	2 tablespoons butter, melted
1 1/2 teaspoons honey	1/2 cup firmly packed light
1 1/2 teaspoons ground cinnamon	brown sugar
1 cup milk	1/2 cup chopped pecans
1 teaspoon vanilla extract	2 tablespoons honey

Spray two 13x9-inch glass baking dishes with nonstick cooking spray.

Slice French bread diagonally into 1-inch-thick slices.

In a large bowl, whisk together eggs, honey, and cinnamon. When thoroughly mixed, stir in milk and vanilla. Dip slices into egg mixture, coating both sides. Arrange bread in prepared dishes, cover with plastic wrap, and refrigerate overnight.

Remove pans from refrigerator and uncover 30 minutes before baking. Drizzle melted butter over bread. Sprinkle with sugar and pecans; drizzle honey over top.

Bake at 350 degrees for 20 minutes. Serve with warm maple syrup, if desired.

Bavarian Town
Bed & Breakfast

206 Beyerlein Street
Frankenmuth, MI 48734
517-652-8057

Hosts: Louie and Kathy Weiss

*O*ur modern Cape Cod is located in a quiet residential district just five blocks from downtown Frankenmuth—Michigan's largest tourist attraction. We are German-speaking descendants of the original settlers of Frankenmuth and are happy to share a wealth of local information, including the history of St. Lorenz Church. Each air-conditioned room is beautifully decorated and smoke-free. Bedrooms have private toilets and sinks with a shared shower.

Rates at Bavarian Town Bed & Breakfast range from $50-$70.
Rates include a full breakfast.

Bavarian Ham Strata

This recipe is wonderfully versatile. Crabmeat or shrimp can be substituted for the ham. It can be prepared the night before to serve at that special brunch and reheated or frozen in ramekins for those unexpected walk-in guests.

serves 10-12

20 slices white sandwich bread
 3 cups bite-size pieces
       cooked ham
10 ounces sharp Cheddar
       cheese, shredded
       (approximately 3 cups)
10 ounces Swiss cheese, shredded
       (approximately 3 cups)
 6 eggs
 3 cups whole milk

1/2 teaspoon onion salt
1/2 teaspoon dry mustard
1/2 teaspoon seasoned salt
1/4 teaspoon black pepper

Topping:
 3 cups crushed cornflakes
1/2 cup (1 stick) butter,
       melted

Butter a 13x9-inch pan; set aside.

Remove crusts and slice bread in half; arrange half of the bread in bottom of prepared pan. Place 1 1/2 cups of the ham on top of bread. Combine cheeses and sprinkle half over ham layer. Repeat layers using remaining bread, ham, and cheese.

In a medium bowl, slightly beat eggs. Stir in milk, onion salt, mustard, seasoned salt, and pepper. Pour over layers. Cover pan with foil and refrigerate overnight.

Preheat oven to 350 degrees. Remove foil from pan. Combine cornflakes and butter in a small bowl; mix well. Sprinkle over strata. Bake 60 minutes. Remove from oven and let stand 10 minutes before cutting into squares.

The Birch Haven Inn

219 Leelanau Avenue
PO Box 411
Frankfort, MI 49635
616-352-4008

Hosts: Chris and Amy Hone

The Birch Haven Inn is a 100-year-old Victorian mansion in the lovely Lake Michigan port city of Frankfort. Set high on a hill, there's always a spectacular seasonal view of Lake Michigan. Relax in the luxury of our antique-filled rooms, or walk one block to our white sand beach. It's only two blocks to the quaint shops and restaurants of downtown Frankfort. Canoe, fish, sail, hike, golf, ski, or shop after you enjoy a sumptuous breakfast in our formal dining room.

Rates at The Birch Haven Inn range from $75-$85.
Rates include a full breakfast.

Birch Haven Eggs

This is the easiest and tastiest egg dish you'll ever find. It makes a colorful impression on your guests that they won't soon forget.

makes 4 eggs

4   eggs
4   teaspoons half-and-half
2   tablespoons grated Cheddar cheese
    Salt
    Paprika
2   English muffins
1   large tomato, chopped
2   green onions, chopped

Preheat oven to 350 degrees. Generously spray 4 ramekins with nonstick cooking spray.

Break 1 egg into each ramekin; cover with 1 teaspoon half-and-half, 1/2 tablespoon of the cheese, and a pinch of salt. Sprinkle with paprika. Bake 12-14 minutes, or until eggs are set.

Meanwhile, toast and butter English muffins. Use a large spoon to remove eggs, taking care to keep egg intact. Place 1 egg on each muffin half. Sprinkle tomatoes and onion over each egg. Serve immediately.

Village Park Bed & Breakfast

60 West Park Street
Fruitport, MI 49415
616-865-6289 or 800-469-1118

Host: John Hewett

Village Park Bed & Breakfast is a country classic-style bed and breakfast overlooking Spring Lake and Village Park where guests can picnic, play tennis, or use the pedestrian bike path and boat launch. Spring Lake has access to Lake Michigan and is close to Hoffmaster Park and Gillette Sand Dune Nature Center, which serves the greater Grand Haven and Muskegon area. The Inn is also the historic setting of Mineral Springs Health Resort. Guests can begin the day in the exercise room and relax in the sauna or outdoor hot tub. There are six guest rooms, all with private baths and room air conditioners. Outdoor decks and a relaxing common area complete with fireplace are provided for your enjoyment.

Village Park Bed & Breakfast features home-style breakfasts. VISA and MasterCard are accepted and advance reservations are requested. Special packages are also available.

Rates at Village Park Bed & Breakfast range from $60-$90.
Rates include a full or continental-plus breakfast.

Country Potato Jubilee

The innkeeper's friend and part-time chef created this dish for camping and often serves it with salsa scrambled eggs and fruit.

serves 8

1½ pounds breakfast sausage
 2 packages (32 ounces each) frozen southern-style hash brown potatoes
 2 teaspoons garlic oil
 4 teaspoons butter, divided
 1 tablespoon horseradish
 6 drops of liquid smoke
 1 large onion, chopped

 1 green pepper, chopped
 1 package (8 ounces) grated Co-Jack cheese

Garnish:
   Cherry tomatoes, quartered
   Parsley
   Nasturtium flowers (optional)

Brown sausage in a wok or large, deep frying pan; drain and set aside. Remove drippings from pan. Heat oil in 2 teaspoons of the butter in pan. Add hash browns, cooking for 5 minutes. Add sausage, remaining 2 teaspoons butter, horseradish, liquid smoke, onions, and green peppers. Stir and brown over low heat. Add cheese and blend well. Serve immediately, garnished with cherry tomato quarters, parsley, and nasturtiums.

Will O'Glenn Irish Bed and Breakfast

1286 64th Street
PO Box 288
Glenn, MI 49416
616-227-3045

Hosts: Shelly and Ward Gahan

*E*njoy a warm Irish welcome and the serenity of a 17-acre estate. Will O'Glenn offers four charming guest rooms, each with private bath. The house is full of Irish art, literature, and antiques. Large common areas, decks, and gardens are just a part of this rambling country manor.

Let us tempt you with our authentic full Irish breakfast featuring imported Irish meats and homemade Irish brown bread. Madra, the Irish Wolfhound, will give his own warm (and wet) Irish welcome!

The Inn is located south of Holland between Saugatuck and South Haven—just minutes from Lake Michigan, bike trails, shopping, and fine dining.

Rates at Will O'Glenn Irish Bed and Breakfast range from $89-$109.
Rates include a full breakfast.

Irish Brown Bread

*Irish Brown Bread was especially popular in Ireland when butter was scarce.
The cross, cut into the loaf, is said to bring the blessing of the Father, Son,
and Holy Spirit onto the bread so that none of it would be wasted.
Great with jams or cheese.*

makes 1 loaf

2 cups whole wheat flour
1 cup flour
$1/2$ cup wheat germ
$1/2$ cup oatmeal

1 tablespoon baking soda
1 egg
$2^{1}/2$ cups buttermilk

In a large bowl, combine flours, wheat germ, oatmeal, and baking soda.
Add egg and buttermilk (these ingredients make the dough soft and easy to
handle); blend well. Form into a round loaf and place onto a greased round
cake pan. Cut a deep cross into loaf.

Bake in a 400-degree oven for 20 minutes. Reduce heat to 200 degrees
and bake another 30 minutes.

Highland Park Hotel
Bed and Breakfast

1414 Lake Avenue
Grand Haven, MI 49417
616-846-1473

Hosts: Don and Carol Trumbull

"We overlook nothing but Lake Michigan."

Experience the enchanting nineteenth century cottage colony of Highland Park. Enjoy sand-swept beaches, rambling boardwalks through wooded dunes, and spectacular sunsets. Close to bike paths, golf, cross-country skiing, charter fishing, and downtown Grand Haven.

The Inn has six guest rooms, all with private baths and air-conditioning. Breakfasts are homemade and wonderful.

Rates at Highland Park Hotel Bed and Breakfast range from $70-$110.
Rates include a buffet-style full breakfast.

Baked Eggs

A quick breakfast dish with a delicate taste and appealing appearance. This recipe is good for a buffet and complements other side dishes such as fruit salads, sliced meats, or green vegetables.

serves 6-8

2 tablespoons butter
9 eggs
1/2 cup sour cream
1 teaspoon salt
1/2 cup milk
2 tablespoons chopped green onion

Preheat oven to 325 degrees. Melt butter in an 8x8-inch glass baking dish in oven.

Beat eggs in a medium bowl. Add sour cream, salt, and milk; whisk until creamy. Stir in onions. Pour into baking dish. Bake 35 minutes, or until eggs are firm.

Lakeshore Bed and Breakfast

11001 Lakeshore Drive
Grand Haven, MI 49460
616-844-2697

Hosts: Dan and Jaclyn Hansen

*T*his fully restored 5,000-square-foot mansion was built in 1935 on 275 feet of Lake Michigan beach frontage. Amenities include breathtaking views from each room, beach chairs and umbrellas on the beach, and showers at the overlook. Enjoy our spacious lawn with majestic shade trees, rest in one of our hammocks, or sit on one of the many decks offering views from the Grand Haven Pier to Holland.

We also offer complementary evening aperitifs on weekends, fresh flowers, Jacuzzi bathtubs, air-conditioning, and a gourmet full breakfast. Enjoy our unique collection of historical documents and memorabilia of American presidents. This classic estate exudes charm, style, and ambiance too rich to describe.

Rates at Lakeshore Bed and Breakfast range from $95-$275.
Rates include a gourmet full breakfast.

Eggs Poached in White Wine

Our guests rave about this entree which we serve with fresh fruit. The aroma and smooth texture of this sauce are too rich to describe. Substitute fresh asparagus, when in season, for the crab or to entertain vegetarian guests. Preparation time is under 20 minutes. This recipe also uses wine as a poaching liquid for the eggs. Although any white wine will do, we suggest selecting a Michigan vintage.

serves 2

2 tablespoons butter
3/4 cup white wine
4 eggs
1/4 cup freshly grated Parmesan cheese
4 English muffin halves, toasted and buttered
8 strips crabmeat (2^1/$_2$x^1/$_2$ inches each)

Sauce:
4 tablespoons sour cream
Salt
White pepper
2 teaspoons flour

Melt butter over low heat in a nonstick skillet with glass cover; add wine. Carefully add eggs and sprinkle tops with cheese. Place crab strips in liquid around edge of pan. Cover immediately and cook over low heat until whites are firm. (Do not lift cover until ready to remove eggs.)

Remove eggs, reserving liquid, and place on prepared muffin halves. Place 2 strips of crab over each egg.

Add sour cream to reserved liquid; adjust seasonings with salt and pepper, as desired. Stir until well blended. Add flour and continue to stir over moderate heat until sauce is thick and bubbly, about 1 minute. Pour over eggs and serve immediately.

Coppys Inn

13424 Phal Road
Grass Lake, MI 49240
517-522-4850

Hosts: Willy and Sharon Coppernoll

Coppys Inn is located on a 65-acre farm in Grass Lake, a small town in southwestern Michigan. Our farm is the homestead of the Coppernoll family and will soon be family-owned for 100 years.

Our comfy Inn has five bedrooms, all with private baths, central air, and beautiful countryside views. Our home and the small-town atmosphere of Grass Lake offer relaxation and simple pleasures. We are close to numerous lakes, golf courses, and antique shopping. Warm hospitality awaits the busy traveler or the folks looking for a quiet country getaway.

Rates at Coppys Inn range from $55-$75.
Rates include a full breakfast.

Stuffed French Toast with Apple Syrup

This recipe can be prepared the night before. We like to serve it with fresh fruit and bacon or sausage. Your guests will rave about the warm apple cider syrup.

serves 8

1 loaf (1 pound) French bread, unsliced

1 package (8 ounces) cream cheese, cubed

8 eggs

2¹/2 cups milk, light cream or half-and-half

6 tablespoons butter or margarine, melted

1/4 cup maple syrup

Syrup:

1/2 cup sugar

4 teaspoons cornstarch

1/2 teaspoon ground cinnamon

1 tablespoon lemon juice

1 cup apple cider or apple juice

2 tablespoons butter or margarine

Cut French bread into cubes (about 12 cups).

Grease a 13x9-inch baking dish. Place half of the bread cubes in prepared dish. Top with cream cheese cubes and remaining bread cubes.

In a blender or bowl with electric mixer, combine eggs, milk, butter, and syrup until well blended. Pour mixture evenly over bread cubes. Using a spatula, lightly press layers to evenly moisten bread. Cover with plastic wrap and refrigerate overnight.

Preheat oven to 325 degrees. Bake 40-45 minutes, or until center appears set and sides are lightly browned. Let stand 10 minutes before serving.

To make syrup, in a small saucepan, stir together sugar, cornstarch, and cinnamon. Stir in lemon juice and cider. Cook and stir mixture over medium heat until thick and bubbly; cook 2 minutes longer. Stir in butter and serve warm with French toast.

The Hanson House

604 Peninsular Street
Grayling, MI 49738
517-348-6630

Hosts: Dave and Jill Wyman

A lumber baron's gift to his wife, our Victorian home still retains its original grandeur. Enjoy ornately carved woodwork and staircase, leaded and stained glass beveled windows, three carved fireplaces with Roman tile, and decorative 1882 wall murals depicting scenes of the Danish countryside. There are four guest rooms (two with private baths), a bridal suite, period furnishings, and a Victorian turret. The Au Sable and Manistee Rivers are close by along with many lakes for canoeing, fishing, swimming, and boating. Golf, downhill and cross-country skiing are also available. Visit The Icehouse Quilt Shop, just three blocks away, selected as one of the top ten quilt shops in North America. Relax and enjoy the quiet atmosphere and home-cooked breakfasts. We are one and a half miles from I-75 and open year-round.

Rates at The Hanson House range from $65-$75.
Rates include a full breakfast.

Blueberry French Toast Cobbler

Breakfast receives rave revues when this popular French toast variation is served. This recipe is easy to make and can be prepared ahead of time, saving precious minutes the following morning. It not only smells and tastes great, but is beautiful when presented at the table. Leftovers can easily be reheated for those late-sleeping guests. If fresh blueberries are not available, substitute frozen apples, blueberries, or peaches, unthawed.

serves 6-8

1 loaf French bread	1 teaspoon cinnamon
5 eggs	1 teaspoon cornstarch
1/2 cup milk	4 1/2 cups (1 1/2 pounds)
1/4 teaspoon baking powder	blueberries
1 teaspoon vanilla extract	2 tablespoons butter, melted
1/2 cup sugar (use less if berries are sweet)	Confectioners' sugar

Slice bread into eight, 3/4-inch-thick slices; arrange in a shallow baking pan.

In a medium bowl, whisk together eggs, milk, baking powder, and vanilla. Pour over bread, turning to coat evenly. Cover with plastic wrap and let stand 2 hours at room temperature or overnight in refrigerator.

Preheat oven to 450 degrees. Spray a 13x9-inch baking pan with nonstick cooking spray.

Mix sugar, cinnamon and cornstarch in a medium bowl; gently fold in blueberries until well coated. Spread blueberries in prepared pan; place egg-soaked bread, wettest side up, on berries, wedging slices in tightly. Brush tops of bread with butter and bake 20-25 minutes until toast is golden and berries are bubbling around edge of pan. To serve, place toast on plates; spoon blueberry sauce from bottom of pan over top and sprinkle with confectioners' sugar.

The Thistle Inn

300 North 152nd Avenue
Holland, MI 49424
616-399-0409

Hosts: Gary and Pat Teske

The Thistle Inn is located close to Lake Michigan on the north side of Holland, Michigan. The area is best known for its annual Tulip Time festivities in May with authentic Dutch customs and sites. The Inn offers guest rooms with private baths, air-conditioning, TV, in-room coffee and tea, and individual walk-outs to the patio and hot tub.

Rates at The Thistle Inn range from $75-$85.
Rates include a full breakfast.

Thistle Inn Crepes

Since Holland is in the center of one of the largest blueberry producing areas of the country, this recipe is a perfect way to enjoy locally grown fruit. Both crepes and filling can be prepared in advance. Crepes can be frozen for several months and thawed at room temperature in about an hour. Prepare this recipe when fruits are in season or use any variety of canned fruits.

makes 22 crepes

Crepes:
- 1 1/2 cups milk
- 1 1/4 cups flour
- 2 tablespoons sugar
- 3 eggs
- 2 tablespoons butter, melted
- Dash of salt

Filling:
- 2 cups blueberries
- 1/4 cup light corn syrup
- 1 1/4 cups water, divided
- 5 tablespoons sugar
- 2 1/2 tablespoons cornstarch
- 1 teaspoon lemon juice
- Dash of cinnamon
- 2-3 peaches, peeled and sliced

Combine milk, flour, sugar, eggs, butter, and salt in a medium bowl; beat until well blended. Lightly spray a 5- to 6-inch crepe pan or skillet with nonstick cooking spray. Heat entire surface of pan; remove from heat and add 2 tablespoons batter. Tilt pan to spread batter; return to heat. When edges are slightly dry and underside is light brown, turn and cook for about 30 seconds more. Invert crepe onto paper towel; repeat process until all crepes are cooked. Cool; and stack with paper towel between each one.

Combine blueberries, corn syrup, cinnamon, and 1 cup water in a medium pan; cook over medium heat until well blended and heated through. In a small bowl, mix together cornstarch, sugar, remaining 1/4 cup water, and lemon juice. Gradually add to pan, stirring until mixture comes to a boil. Continue stirring a few more minutes until cornstarch is clear and mixture is thick. Remove from heat; add peaches and cool.

To serve, warm crepes between paper towels in microwave on low for approximately 20 seconds. Spoon warm or cool filling down center of crepe. Roll crepe and place seam side down on plate. Garnish with whipped topping, if desired.

Holly Crossing
Bed & Breakfast

304 South Saginaw Street
Holly, MI 48442
810-634-7075

Hosts: Carl and Nicole Cooper

The stately turn-of-the-century Queen Anne house at Holly Crossing, now a charming Inn, stands on the border of Holly's Olde Towne. A popular tourist attraction, this nineteenth century railroad boomtown offers antiquing, dining, entertainment, and festivals all within two blocks of the Inn. The Inn's five beautiful bedrooms, all with private bathrooms, await your visit. Choose our honeymoon suite with balcony, fireplace, and Jacuzzi or a deluxe Jacuzzi room complete with queen-size beds. Breakfast-to-your-door and champagne are included. Other guest rooms have full-size beds and include breakfast in the dining room. We also provide a smoke-free environment for the benefit of our guests.

Rates at Holly Crossing Bed & Breakfast range from $59-$169.
Rates include a full breakfast.

Breakfast Casserole

This recipe is quick and easy to make. Prepared the night before and baked the following morning, it's perfect for an Inn-full of guests! Serve with fresh fruit and raisin toast with apple butter for a memorable treat. Substitute cooked diced ham or crisp crumbled bacon for sausage. Cut into eight pieces (hearty enough to fill one of Holly's railroad linemen) or cut into 12 smaller pieces (for the less hearty appetite). It is easy to reheat leftovers.

serves 8

1¹/2 to 2	pounds bulk sausage
8	large eggs
2¹/2	cups milk
1	teaspoon dry mustard
1	pound grated Cheddar cheese, divided
3 to 4	cups square-cut croutons
1	can (4 ounces) mushrooms (optional)

Brown sausage in a medium skillet, stirring to crumble meat; drain well.

Beat eggs, milk, and mustard in a medium bowl; stir in half the cheese and mix to blend.

Spray a 13x9-inch baking pan with nonstick cooking spray. Cover bottom of prepared pan with croutons and sprinkle with cooked sausage. Pour egg mixture over top and add mushrooms, if desired. Top with remaining half of cheese. Cover with plastic wrap and refrigerate overnight.

Bake uncovered in a 350-degree oven for 45-50 minutes until middle of casserole is set. Let stand 5 minutes before slicing.

Charleston House
Historic Inn

918 College Avenue
Houghton, MI 49931
800-482-7404

Hosts: John and Helen Sullivan

This romantic home was built in the early 1900s by Allen Rees, a prominent Houghton attorney. Ornate woodwork, stained leaded glass windows, a large library with fireplace, and a grand interior staircase are just a few of the striking features in this Inn. A double veranda with ceiling fans and wicker furniture complete this turn-of-the-century Georgian house located in the historic district within walking distance of MTU campus and downtown. There are comfortable reproduction furnishings including a king-size canopy bed and queen and twin posturepedics. All spacious guest rooms have air-conditioning, cable TV, telephones, ceiling fans, and sitting areas. A refrigerator and microwave are also available for guests' use. Children are always welcome, but pets must remain at home. Smoking is permitted in the garden.

Rates at Charleston House Historic Inn range from $78-$110.
Rates include a full buffet breakfast.

Finnish Pancake with Raspberry Sauce

You can watch this pancake puff up while baking, then fall when removed from the oven. Although our guests love this Raspberry Sauce, you can sub-stitute your favorite topping, use fresh fruit, or fruit-flavored syrups.

makes one 13x9-inch pan

6 eggs	Raspberry Sauce:
3/4 cup flour	1 cup sugar
1 teaspoon vanilla extract	2 tablespoons cornstarch
1/4 teaspoon salt	1 cup water
1 cup (8 ounces) evaporated milk	1/2 cup fresh or frozen raspberries, drained
3 cups milk (whole or skim)	
4 tablespoons butter	

Preheat oven to 425 degrees.

In a blender, mix eggs, flour, vanilla, salt, evaporated milk, and whole milk.

Melt butter in a 13x9-inch pan in oven. Pour contents of blender into pre-pared pan and bake 15 minutes; reduce temperature to 375 degrees and bake 20 minutes more.

To make sauce, mix sugar and cornstarch in a medium saucepan. Cook over medium heat. Add water and whisk, stirring constantly until thickened. Remove from heat; fold in berries. Serve warm over pancake.

Union Hill Inn
Bed & Breakfast

306 Union Street
Ionia, MI 48846
616-527-0955

Hosts: Tom and Mary Kay Moular

*U*nion Hill Inn is an elegant 1868 Italianate-style home built by Civil War Captain Lucius Mills. During the war it served as a former station for the underground railroad. The rooms are beautifully furnished with antiques. Enjoy the living area with fireplace, piano, porcelain village, and porcelain dolls. Relax in the upstairs sitting room, or watch cable TV in your room. Flower beds surround this home noted for its expansive veranda and panoramic view overlooking the community— only two blocks from historic downtown. With all the beauty at Union Hill Inn, the greatest thing you will experience is the love and peace that abide here.

Rates at Union Hill Inn Bed & Breakfast range from $50-$75.
Rates include a full breakfast.

Asparagus Ham Quiche

This recipe is extremely easy to make as it has a self-rising crust. It can be doubled or tripled for a larger group. It is simple to change the recipe by adding spinach, broccoli, or your favorite ingredient. It also freezes well.

serves 6

    1 package (10 ounces) frozen cut asparagus, thawed
    8 ounces cooked ham, chopped
    4 ounces Swiss cheese, shredded (1 cup)
 1/4 cup chopped onion
    3 eggs
    1 cup milk
 3/4 cup Bisquick
 1/8 teaspoon black pepper

Preheat oven to 375 degrees. Spray a 9-inch pie plate with nonstick cooking spray.

Layer asparagus, ham, cheese, and onion in prepared pan.

Beat eggs in a medium bowl; add milk, Bisquick, and pepper. Pour over asparagus mixture. Bake 35-45 minutes, or until knife inserted in center comes out clean. Cool 5 minutes; cut and serve.

Bon Accord Farm
Bed and Breakfast

532 East Polk Road
Ithaca, MI 48847
517-875-3136

Hosts: Richard and JoAnn Allen

*B*eautiful woods such as oak, maple, butternut, ash, walnut, cherry, and pine combine to give this 1872 farmhouse charm and comfort. Most of the trees were cut from our own woods and then shaped, carved, and finished by local craftsmen and six generations of Allens.

Breakfast is reminiscent of when the reputation of a farm family was based on the cleanliness of the fields, the health of the livestock, and the meals served to family, guests, and visiting threshers.

With 1000 acres of fields, woods, and meadows to enjoy, it's a peaceful place to relax, read, or sit under a tree and watch the world go by.

Rates at Bon Accord Farm Bed and Breakfast range from $48-$58.
Rates include a full breakfast.

Tomato-Basil Frittata

Delicious served with candied yams and sausages! Scallions may be
substituted for the sweet onion.

serves 4-5

2 tablespoons butter, divided
1 medium sweet onion, thinly
   sliced
1/4 cup sweet red pepper,
   chopped
6-8 large eggs
1/2 cup plain nonfat yogurt
1 medium tomato, seeded and
   finely chopped

1/4 cup finely chopped fresh
   basil
Salt and pepper
1 cup shredded Monterey-Jack
   cheese
1 cup shredded sharp Cheddar
   cheese
1/4 cup freshly grated Parmesan
   cheese

Melt 1 tablespoon of the butter in a 10- to 12-inch skillet. Add onion and cook over medium heat until softened, about 1 minute. Add red pepper and continue to cook 1 more minute; set aside.

Beat eggs in a medium bowl; blend in yogurt. Add tomato and basil; adjust seasonings with salt and pepper, as desired.

Add remaining 1 tablespoon butter to skillet. Pour egg mixture over onions and peppers. Cook over medium heat, making sure ingredients are evenly distributed in pan. As eggs are cooking, lift with spatula, allowing uncooked portion to flow underneath. Remove from heat once eggs are softly set.

Mix cheeses and generously sprinkle over top of frittata. Place skillet under broiler until cheese is lightly browned. To serve, slice in pie-shaped wedges.

The Munro House
Bed & Breakfast

202 Maumee
Jonesville, MI 49250
517-849-9292

Hostess: Joyce Yarde

Visit the elegance of a bygone era in this 1840 Greek Revival structure built by George C. Munro, a brigadier general during the Civil War. Visitors can see the secret room used to hide runaway slaves as part of the underground railway. The seven cozy guest rooms are furnished with period antiques, many with working fireplaces and Jacuzzis. The Inn has lots of common areas for guests to enjoy, such as a hearth fireplace and large parlor with grand piano. The award-winning Orange-Vanilla French Toast is just one of the many hearty breakfasts that are featured. The Munro House Bed & Breakfast is one block south of U.S. 12 in downtown Jonesville.

Rates at The Munro House Bed & Breakfast range from $56-$150.
Rates include a full breakfast.

Orange-Vanilla French Toast

Soaking the bread overnight is what gives this toast its wonderful rich taste. It's ideal for brunches and extended breakfast times. Baked French toast will keep two hours in a warm oven in a foil-covered pan with corners turned up to allow steam to escape.

serves 4

6 eggs
3/4 cup orange juice
3/4 cup half-and-half or
    evaporated milk
2 tablespoons vanilla extract
1/4 cup sugar
1 loaf bread, cut into 8 thick
    slices, ends removed

Orange Apricot Syrup:
2 cups orange marmalade
2 cups apricot preserves
1/4 cup sugar
1/4 cup orange juice

Spray a 13x9-inch pan with nonstick cooking spray.

In a large bowl, whisk eggs. Add orange juice, half-and-half, vanilla, and sugar; whisk until well mixed. Dip each slice of bread in mixture, coating both sides; place in prepared pan. Pour remaining mixture over bread. Cover pan and refrigerate overnight.

To cook, fry or grill slowly (250 degrees on electric skillet) until golden brown on both sides, about 10 minutes per side. Before serving, sprinkle confectioners' sugar on top of toast and serve with warm Orange Apricot Syrup.

To make syrup, mix marmalade, preserves, sugar, and orange juice in a medium saucepan; simmer 5 minutes.

Hall House Bed & Breakfast

106 Thompson Street
Kalamazoo, MI 49006
616-343-2500

Hosts: Jerry and Joanne Hofferth

*H*all House is a 75-year-old Georgian Revival home located in the National Historic District on the edge of the Kalamazoo College campus. The 14-room home has five guest rooms/suites which can accommodate from two to five guests. All rooms have private baths (some with soaking tubs, Jacuzzis, and fireplaces), cable TV, telephones, and air-conditioning. Polished mahogany woodwork; marble stairs, pewabic tile entryway, domed dining room ceiling, and a hand-painted mural in the library are just some of the exceptional features of the home. Theater, restaurants, antiques, and golf are nearby, and complementary refreshments are served each afternoon.

Rates at Hall House Bed & Breakfast range from $85-$140.
Rates include a continental plus breakfast weekdays and a
full breakfast on weekends.

Quick Blueberry Cobbler

If you are short of time, this is the cobbler to make. It takes very little preparation, and you can have a homemade fresh cobbler in less than an hour. We serve it warm with a pitcher of cream on the side.

serves 6-8

¹/₂ cup (1 stick) butter or margarine
1 cup flour
1 cup sugar
1 teaspoon baking powder
¹/₂ cup milk
2 cups blueberries or raspberries
¹/₃ cup sugar

Melt butter in a 10- or 11-inch long rectangular glass baking dish in a pre-heated 350-degree oven.

Mix together flour, sugar, and baking powder in a medium bowl. Add milk to flour mixture; stir just until moistened. Spoon batter over melted butter.

In a small bowl, gently mix blueberries and sugar; pour over batter. Bake 30-35 minutes. (Crust will rise to the top while baking.) Serve warm.

Stuart Avenue Inn

229 Stuart Avenue
Kalamazoo, MI 49007
800-461-0621

Hosts: Tom and Mary Lou Baker

*S*tuart Avenue Inn is a wonderful collection of Victorian homes and award-winning gardens located in the prestigious Stuart Area Historic District. Operating since 1983, the Inn includes the Bartlett-Upjohn House, Chappell House, Carriage House, and McDuffee Gardens. The buildings are splendid examples of architecture which spans the 1880s to the turn of the century. Each building has been restored with guest rooms that are classically appointed with fine hand-printed art wallpapers, Belgian lace curtains, and period antiques. All Inn rooms have private baths, cable television, telephones, and air-conditioning. Many guest rooms also have fireplaces, wet bars, and several have double-Jacuzzi spas; but rest assured, all Inn rooms are private and romantic.

Rates at Stuart Avenue Inn range from $49-$150.
Rates include a continental breakfast.

Classic Cream Scones

These scones are classically delicious. For something different,
try substituting a variety of dried fruit or currants.

makes 8 scones

2 cups flour
1/3 cup sugar
1 1/2 teaspoons baking powder
1/2 teaspoon baking soda
1/4 teaspoon salt
6 tablespoons butter, chilled
1/2 cup heavy whipping cream
1 large egg
1 1/2 teaspoons vanilla extract
2/3 cup dried cherries, chopped

Preheat oven to 400 degrees.

In a large bowl, stir together flour, sugar, baking powder, baking soda, and salt. Slice butter into 1/2-inch cubes and cut into flour using a pastry blender until mixture resembles coarse crumbs.

Stir together whipping cream, egg, and vanilla in a small bowl. Add to flour mixture and combine. Stir in dried cherries.

With lightly floured hands, pat dough into an 8-inch diameter circle on an ungreased baking sheet. (Dough will be slightly sticky.) Cut into 8 wedges with a serrated knife.

Bake 18-20 minutes, or until top is lightly browned and a wooden pick inserted in center of scone comes out clean. Remove from baking sheet and put on wire rack; cool 5 minutes. Serve warm or cool completely and store in an airtight container.

Belknap's Garnet House

238 County Road
Kearsarge, MI 49942
906-337-5607

Hosts: Howard and Debby Belknap

*B*elknap's Garnet House is an authentic century-old Victorian home built for a mining captain during the 1800s copper rush in Keweenaw Peninsula. The three-acre grounds include a windmill, root cellar, ice house, carriage house, and oftentimes a visiting bear or two! Original fireplaces, leaded and beveled glass windows, pantries, fixtures, woodwork, and a huge porch contribute to this lovely but comfortable Inn furnished with period antiques. Three guest rooms are available, each with their own private bath; two separate guest rooms share a bath. Visit nearby historic Calumet, local mines, lighthouses, and Copper Harbor. The Inn has been featured in *U.S. News and World Report*'s "Great Vacation Drives" and *Midwest Living* magazine.

Rates at Belknap's Garnet House range from $60-$90.
Rates include a full breakfast.

Zucchini and Mushroom Frittata

This recipe is so versatile that it can be prepared the night before or just before baking. It can also be frozen, once assembled. Simply remove from the freezer, thaw, and bake. Great to have on hand when you get too busy!
Serve with your favorite warmed salsa.

serves 8

10 eggs
1/2 cup flour
 1 teaspoon salt
 1 teaspoon baking powder
 1 carton (16 ounces) cottage cheese
1/2 cup (1 stick) butter, melted, divided
 2 medium zucchini, peeled and chopped
 1 pint fresh mushrooms, sliced
 1 can (4 ounces) mild green chiles

Preheat oven to 350 degrees. Spray a 13x9-inch baking pan with nonstick cooking spray.

Beat eggs in a large bowl; add flour, salt, baking powder, cottage cheese, and 1/4 cup of the butter. Mix until well blended.

Heat remaining 1/4 cup butter in a large skillet. Saute squash and mushrooms; cool 5 minutes. Add vegetables and butter to egg mixture; stir to mix. Add chiles. Pour into prepared pan; bake 1 hour, or until eggs are set.

Serve hot frittata directly from pan or cut into individual squares. Top with warmed salsa, if desired.

Laurium Manor Inn

320 Tamarack Street
Laurium, MI 49913
906-337-2549

Hosts: Dave and Julie Sprenger

*L*aurium Manor Inn is a spectacular 13,000-square-foot copper baron's neo-classic mansion. Built in 1908 and listed on the National Register of Historic Places, the Inn has ten guest rooms (eight with private baths), two dining rooms, a library, den, parlor, carriage house, and ballroom. Unique features include gilded elephant hide/leather wall coverings, wall murals, gilded marble and tile fireplaces, a private balcony, and wraparound porch with tile floor. All rooms are individually decorated with period antiques. Experience the opulence of this rare home.

Rates at Laurium Manor Inn range from $49-$119.
Rates include a full breakfast.

Glazed Poppy Seed Muffins

This recipe can easily be doubled. Bake both batches according to instructions and freeze what won't be needed. Frozen muffins can be thawed at room temperature and will taste just like freshly baked.

makes 12 muffins

1 1/2 cups flour
3/4 cup milk
1/2 teaspoon vanilla extract
1 1/4 cups sugar
1/2 cup oil
1 teaspoon almond extract
2 eggs
1 teaspoon baking powder
1 tablespoon poppy seeds

Glaze:
3/4 cup powdered sugar
1/4 cup orange juice
1 tablespoon butter or
    margarine, melted
1/2 teaspoon almond extract
    Slivered almonds (optional)

Preheat oven to 350 degrees. Line muffin tins with paper liners.

Combine flour, milk, vanilla, sugar, oil, almond extract, eggs, baking powder, and poppy seeds in a large bowl; mix until well blended. Fill muffin cups 3/4 full with batter. Bake 20-25 minutes.

Meanwhile, prepare glaze by mixing powdered sugar, orange juice, butter, and almond extract in a small bowl; blend until smooth. Remove muffins from oven; poke several holes in tops with a fork. Pour about 1 tablespoon glaze over each muffin; top with almonds, if desired. Remove from pan and cool completely before serving.

The Lamplighter
Bed and Breakfast

602 East Ludington Avenue
Ludington, MI 49431
616-843-9792 or 800-301-9792

Hosts: Judy and Heinz Bertram

*L*ocated only minutes from long stretches of beautiful white sandy beaches and Michigan's most beautiful state park, The Lamplighter is the bed and breakfast of choice for travelers who want to step back in time without losing touch with today.

Judy and Heinz have blended the centennial architecture of their home with their own beautiful collection of European antiques, original paintings, and objects d'art to create a unique ambiance of warmth, comfort, and elegance. Your stay includes a gourmet full breakfast served in the formal dining room or outdoors in the gazebo.

Rates at The Lamplighter Bed and Breakfast range from $75-$125.
Rates include a gourmet full breakfast.

Granola Waffles

These waffles have a delicious flavor and texture. The batter can be frozen in small plastic containers and thawed overnight in the refrigerator. This way waffles may be served quickly on busy mornings, and you can avoid the extra cleanup from preparation. (Batter may be thick after freezing; just add a few tablespoons of milk to thin.)

makes 8 waffles

2 cups 2% milk
2 cups granola (without dried fruit)
2 eggs
1/2 cup (1 stick) margarine, melted

1/4 teaspoon vanilla extract
2 cups flour
1 tablespoon baking powder
1/2 teaspoon baking soda
1/4 teaspoon salt

In a medium bowl, pour milk over granola; stir and let stand 30 minutes. Add eggs and margarine; beat until well blended.

Combine flour, baking powder, baking soda, and salt in a large bowl. Add egg mixture and mix thoroughly with an electric hand mixer or spatula.

Lightly spray waffle iron with nonstick cooking spray. Heat to proper temperature; ladle about 1/2- to 3/4-cup batter into center of iron. Close top; batter will spread over entire grid. (Lid will raise slightly during baking.) Check after about 3 or 4 minutes; waffle is done if golden brown in color. (For a crunchy waffle, wait until steaming stops to remove from iron.)

Serve with Michigan warm maple syrup.

The National House Inn

102 South Parkview
Marshall, MI 49068
616-781-7374

Hostess: Barbara Bradley

*T*he destination of choice...restored in 1976, The National House Inn has taken its rightful position on the National Register of Historic Places. With 16 guest rooms that range in decor from the elegant Victorian Ketchum Suite to the romantic French-country H. C. Brooks Room, the Inn is as welcome to today's visitors as it was to the stage-coach travelers of more than 150 years ago.

You can choose a quiet corner and a good book to curl up with or have a steaming cup of coffee while viewing our beautiful gardens from the porch. A crackling fire, comfortable conversation, and freshly popped popcorn are a few of the simple pleasures that await you when you make it a point to stay with us. Come and see why those who stay once...return again and again.

Rates at The National House Inn range from $68-$130.
Rates include a full (meatless) breakfast.

Sam Hill Sour Cream Cake

This is one of my quick-and-easy favorites—it mixes together really fast and takes little time to bake and serve. The ingredients are in any pantry, so it is a good last minute choice too—even as an evening dessert item. Strawberries are my preference as a topping, but any fresh fruit such as peaches or blueberries is just as pleasing.

makes one 8x8-inch cake

¹/4 cup graham cracker crumbs
¹/4 cup (¹/2 stick) butter
¹/3 cup sugar
2 eggs
¹/2 cup milk
3/4 cup flour
1 teaspoon grated lemon zest

Topping:
¹/2 cup sugar
2 cups sour cream
Fresh sliced strawberries

Preheat oven to 350 degrees. Sprinkle sides and bottom of a greased 8-inch cake pan with graham cracker crumbs. Cream butter and sugar in a small bowl. Beat in eggs, one at a time. Add milk, flour, and lemon zest; blend well.

Pour batter into prepared pan and bake 10 minutes, or until wooden pick inserted in center comes out clean. Turn cake onto serving plate and cool.

To make topping, mix together sugar and sour cream in a small bowl. Spoon into center of cake; arrange strawberries over top in a pattern. Refrigerate until serving.

Hackley-Holt House

523 West Clay Avenue
Muskegon, MI 49440
616-725-7303

Hosts: Bill and Nancy Stone

Sample the Old World charm of the Victorian era in a relaxed and friendly atmosphere. This beautiful Italianate-style house located in the historic district was built in 1857 and is listed on the National and State Register of Historic Places. Enjoy the comfort of the fireplace in the parlor and a book from the library, or relax on the wraparound porch and savor a gourmet full breakfast. For fun, we are within walking distance of downtown parks, shopping, theaters, museums, and the arena. Fine dining, Lake Michigan beaches, state and amusement parks are a short drive away.

Rates at Hackley-Holt House range from $55-$65.
Rates include a gourmet full breakfast.

Swedish Pancakes

This traditional recipe for Swedish crepes has been handed down over the years and featured as the highlight of breakfast buffets served at the Vasa Country Club of Detroit since 1925. They are especially wonderful with lingonberries (imported from Sweden or Finland) as a topping, but can also be served with butter and syrup, powdered sugar, or your favorite fruit topping.

serves 6

2¹/4 cups flour	7 large eggs
2 tablespoons sugar	¹/2 cup (1 stick) butter or
1¹/4 teaspoons salt	margarine for frying
4 cups milk	Lingonberries

Stir together flour, sugar, and salt in a large bowl. Using a wire whisk, gradually add milk; beat until smooth. Add eggs one at a time; beat with wire whisk after each addition. Let batter stand 30 minutes (this will keep pancake intact when flipped). Stir again before cooking.

Heat an 8- to 9-inch skillet over medium heat. Grease pan well using butter or margarine. Measure approximately ¹/3 cup of batter and pour into hot skillet; roll pan to spread batter evenly. Cook until bottom is golden brown and top is starting to bubble. Using a spatula, carefully flip pancake and continue to cook until golden brown. Roll pancake and transfer to a large serving platter. (To keep pancakes warm until all batter is used, place on a serving platter in a 200-degree oven.)

Serve Swedish Pancakes with traditional lingonberry topping.

Port City Victorian Inn

1259 Lakeshore Drive
Muskegon, MI 49441
616-759-0205 or 800-274-3574

Hosts: Fred and Barbara Schossau

Port City Victorian Inn is an 1877 romantic Victorian getaway located on the bluffs of Muskegon Lake, just minutes from Lake Michigan beaches, state parks, downtown theaters, restaurants, and a sports arena.

This five-bedroom home features suites with lake views and private double-whirlpool baths. One guest room is furnished in a nautical theme, while other rooms are elegantly decorated with the flair of the Victorian era. The entire main floor serves as the common area for our guests' enjoyment.

All rooms have air-conditioning, cable TV, phone jacks/computer-modem ready, and desks. A fax is also available. Port City Victorian Inn is open year-round and accepts all major credit cards.

Rates at Port City Victorian Inn range from $65-$125.
Rates include a full breakfast.

Baked Eggs in Basil Sauce

Prepare this recipe during the summer and use basil from your garden or farm market for that fresh-from-the-garden flavor. The combination of butter, milk, and mozzarella gives the sauce a rich and creamy quality.

serves 4

3 tablespoons margarine or
    butter
2 tablespoons flour
1/4 teaspoon salt
1/8 teaspoon black pepper
1/4 cup fresh basil leaves, or
    1 tablespoon dried basil

1 cup milk
4 eggs
1/4 cup mozzarella cheese,
    shredded
Fresh basil leaves for garnish

Preheat oven to 350 degrees. Spray 4 individual baking dishes with non-stick cooking spray.

In a small saucepan, melt margarine. Stir in flour, salt, and pepper. Add milk all at once; cook and stir over medium heat until thick and bubbly. Continue cooking 1 minute more. Remove from heat; stir in basil.

To assemble, spoon about 2 tablespoons basil sauce into each dish. Gently break egg into center and adjust seasonings with additional salt and pepper, as desired. Spoon remaining sauce over eggs.

Bake 18-20 minutes, or until egg is set. Sprinkle with cheese; let stand until cheese melts. Garnish with basil.

The Candlewyck House
Bed & Breakfast

438 East Lowell
PO Box 392
Pentwater, MI 49449
616-869-5967

Hosts: John and Mary Jo Neidow

*O*ur 1868 farmhouse-style Inn offers a comfortable and unique atmosphere. All six rooms (two with fireplaces) have private baths, air-conditioning, cable TV and are furnished with primitive antiques and Americana and folk art chosen from our gift shop, The Painted Pony Mercantile. Relax on our spacious patio, enjoy a glass of wine by the fireplace, or choose a book from our thousand-volume library.

Walk or ride our bikes to beaches, shops, or pier fishing. The Candlewyck House Bed & Breakfast is featured in *Travel Holiday*, *Grand Rapids Magazine*, and *Corvette Quarterly*. We sponsor the popular Joe Pike Memorial Corvette Extravaganza each year the third weekend in May.

Rates at The Candlewick House Bed & Breakfast range from $70-$99.
Rates include a full breakfast.

Seafood Quiche

This quiche recipe goes together so easily—it's all mixed together in one bowl, yet the results are very elegant and always receive "oohs" and "aahs" from my guests. Seafood quiche is great for a luncheon and can also be served as a light entree.

makes three 9-inch or two deep-dish quiches

4 extra large eggs	1 can (6 ounces) shrimp
1/2 cup mayonnaise	1/2 cup chopped green onions
2 cups milk	1 cup shredded mozzarella
2 tablespoons flour	cheese
1/2 teaspoon seasoning salt	1 cup shredded Cheddar
1/2 teaspoon dry mustard	cheese
3-4 drops red hot sauce	3 unbaked pie shells, or 2
1 can (6 ounces) crabmeat	deep-dish pie shells

Preheat oven to 350 degrees.

In a large bowl, beat eggs, mayonnaise, and milk. Add flour, seasoning salt, mustard, red sauce, crabmeat, shrimp, onions, and cheeses. Stir until well blended.

Pour into pie shells and bake 1 hour, or until knife inserted in center comes out clean. Cool 10 minutes; cut each pie into 5-6 pieces and serve with fruit compote and your favorite muffin.

The Pentwater Inn

180 East Lowell
PO Box 98
Pentwater, MI 49449
616-869-5909

Hosts: Donna and Quintus Renshaw

*T*his beautiful Victorian home, built in 1869, will take you back in time with its original exterior gingerbread and quiet setting in the quaint village of Pentwater on the shores of Lake Michigan. Walk to sandy beaches or to specialty gift and antique shops. Guests and hosts can enjoy socializing in the evening with snacks and beverages in the large parlor.

Romantic weekends with candlelight breakfast and evening beverage and canapes are popular. Your friendly hosts have traveled extensively and have filled the Inn with antiques and English tea pots. Breakfast is served with china and silver to complement the Victorian atmosphere. Each room is filled with antiques and all have private baths.

Excellent golfing, charter fishing, antiques, fine dining, and dunes are nearby. Fruit orchards and asparagus farms abound in Oceana County.

Rates at The Pentwater Inn range from $75-$95.
Rates include a gourmet full breakfast and evening beverage and canape.

Oatmeal Cranberry Scones

These nutty tasting scones are always on hand at The Pentwater Inn, as they freeze beautifully and go well with any beverage. They also are elegant when served as a shortcake with ice cream and fresh fruit for an evening dessert. In England they are often served with clotted cream and jam. Any dried fruit can be substituted for the dried cranberries. White raisins or chopped apricots and sliced almonds add wonderful flavor and texture.

makes 24-30 scones

4 cups flour	1 cup (2 sticks) butter, chilled
1/3 cup sugar	3 cups rolled oats
1 tablespoon baking powder	1 cup dried cranberries
1 teaspoon baking soda	2 cups buttermilk
1 teaspoon salt	

Preheat oven to 375 degrees. Mix flour, sugar, baking powder, baking soda, and salt in a large bowl. Cut in butter until it resembles coarse crumbs. Add oats and cranberries, tossing with a fork to distribute. Add buttermilk and stir with a fork until dough forms a rough ball.

Sprinkle a board with flour and knead dough 6 or 7 times, working lightly. Divide dough into 3 equal balls. Pat each ball into a 1/2-inch-thick circle. Cut each circle in 8 or 10 wedges. Place wedges on a greased baking sheet about 1/2-inch apart. Bake 20-25 minutes, or until lightly browned.

Scones may be frozen, then thawed as needed. After thawing, warm in microwave 35 seconds. Serve with jam and butter or whipped cream and jam.

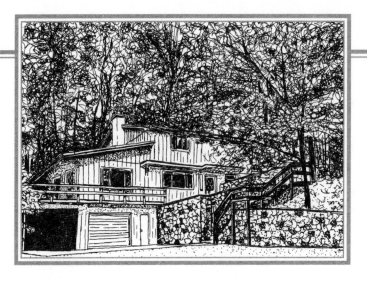

Bear River Valley
Bed & Breakfast

03636 Bear River Road
Petoskey, MI 49770
616-348-2046

Hosts: Russ and Sandra Barkman

Bear River Valley Bed & Breakfast is a northwoods retreat in the heart of Michigan's finest outdoor recreation area. The Inn is close to magnificent lakes and beaches, ski hills and trails, shops, galleries, and fine dining. Tranquility, luxury, and natural beauty greet you. Healthy, whole-grain deluxe continental breakfasts featuring gourmet fare are served in a warm country atmosphere. Guests are invited to enjoy our floor-to-ceiling brick fireplace in the large main room or relax in our Finnish sauna after a full day of activity.

Rates at Bear River Valley Bed & Breakfast range from $65-$75.
Rates include a deluxe continental breakfast.

Maple Pecan Granola

*If you don't have pecans on hand, choose walnuts for the same good,
nutty texture. This recipe doubles easily and keeps well in the refrigerator.
It's nice to have on hand for something "extra special" to present
with breakfast.*

makes 6 cups

3 cups regular oats	2 teaspoons sesame seeds
1/4 cup firmly packed brown sugar	1/2 cup chopped pecans
1/4 cup plus 2 tablespoons wheat germ	1/4 cup nonfat dry milk
1/4 cup flaked coconut	1/4 cup maple syrup
	1/4 cup canola oil
	2 tablespoons maple flavoring

Preheat oven to 350 degrees. Spread oats in a 14x12-inch baking pan;
bake for about 10 minutes.

In a large bowl, combine sugar, wheat germ, coconut, sesame seeds,
pecans, and milk. Add toasted oats.

Combine syrup, oil, and maple flavoring in a small bowl. Add to oat mixture. Stir well to coat ingredients. Pour into pan and bake 20-25 minutes, or
until lightly toasted, stirring twice during baking. Remove from oven. When
cool, store in an airtight container.

Montgomery Place
Bed and Breakfast

618 East Lake Street
Petoskey, MI 49770
616-347-1338

Hosts: Ruth Bellissimo and Diane Gillette

Northwest Michigan...home to Mackinac Island and its name-sake, the Mighty Mac, the longest suspension bridge in North America; and Sleeping Bear Dunes; and Sault Ste. Marie and her seaway locks; and hills and vales; picturesque little towns; and glistening lakes and sandy beaches; and the 117-year-old Montgomery Place Bed and Breakfast, a magnificently preserved Victorian home sitting on a hillside in Petoskey overlooking Lake Michigan's Little Traverse Bay. Close to shops, galleries, and all vacation activities, Montgomery Place features four large comfortable rooms, private baths, a full country breakfast, and afternoon wine and snacks. It seems like Norman Rockwell lives right around the corner.

Rates at Montgomery Place Bed and Breakfast range from $95-$135.
Rates include a gourmet full breakfast.

Breakfast Sausage Squares

This recipe is easy to make and can be assembled the day before. It is a welcome change from the many egg-based dishes.

serves 8

1 pound bulk pork sausage	1 package (10 ounces) frozen
1/2 cup finely chopped onions	chopped spinach, thawed
1/4 teaspoon black pepper	and squeezed dry
3 eggs, slightly beaten	3/4 cup (1 1/2 sticks) butter,
1/4 cup grated Parmesan cheese	melted
1 cup grated mozzarella cheese	10 sheets frozen phyllo dough,
1 container (16 ounces) cottage	thawed
cheese	1/2 cup sour cream for garnish

Brown sausage and onion together in a large skillet until sausage is cooked through and crumbly and onion is transparent. Remove from heat. Add pepper, eggs, cheeses, and spinach to skillet. Mix thoroughly and set aside.

Lightly butter bottom of a 13x9-inch baking pan. Using a pastry brush, butter 5 sheets of the phyllo dough; fold in half and place in prepared pan (there should be 10 layers). Spread sausage mixture evenly over dough. Repeat procedure with remaining 5 sheets phyllo dough, placing them to cover the sausage mixture. (Pan may be covered and refrigerated overnight at this point.)

Bake uncovered at 375 degrees for 45 minutes, or until golden brown. Cut into 8 squares to serve. Garnish with sour cream, if desired.

Serenity—A Bed & Breakfast

504 Rush Street
Petoskey, MI 49770
616-347-6171

Hosts: Ralph and Sherry Gillett

Serenity, our charming turn-of-the century Victorian home, awaits you as you travel to northern Michigan. We offer warm hospitality, casual elegance, and hearty, homemade breakfasts.

Our three guest rooms (two are air-conditioned), each with its own private bath, are furnished with antiques creating a gracious charm.

Our guests enjoy our glass-enclosed porches, which are furnished with wicker. We are within walking distance of the Gaslight District, fine restaurants, a beautiful waterfront park, and are only 35 miles from Mackinac Island.

Rates at Serenity—A Bed & Breakfast range from $70-$85.
Rates include a full breakfast.

Orange Scones

Steep a fresh pot of tea and wait for the scones to finish baking!
The fresh flavor of warm scones topped with Orange Spread
complements any breakfast table or afternoon tea cart.

makes 6 scones

1³/4 cups flour
3 tablespoons sugar
2¹/2 teaspoons baking powder
¹/3 cup cold margarine
¹/2 cup raisins
2 teaspoons grated orange peel
2 eggs, divided and beaten
4-6 tablespoons milk

Orange Spread:
¹/4 cup (¹/2 stick) margarine, softened
2 tablespoons orange marmalade

Preheat oven to 400 degrees.

Mix together flour, sugar, and baking powder. Cut in margarine using fork or pastry blender until mixture resembles coarse crumbs. Stir in raisins, orange peel, 1 of the eggs, and enough milk to moisten. Turn dough onto lightly floured surface and knead 10 times. Roll or pat into an 8-inch circle and cut into 6 wedges.

Beat remaining egg in a small bowl. Place wedges on ungreased cookie sheet and brush with egg. Bake 10 minutes until lightly browned. Immediately remove from cookie sheet. Place on wire rack to cool.

To make spread, combine margarine and marmalade in a small bowl; mix until well blended. Serve with Orange Scones.

The Chestnut House
Bed & Breakfast

1911 Lakeshore Drive
St. Joseph, MI 49085
616-983-7413

Hosts: Frank and Elizabeth Care

*L*et our elegantly furnished and distinctively decorated home over-looking Lake Michigan be your romantic getaway. The Old World English charm will delight you as you're pampered and served a scrumptious full breakfast in our solarium or evening hors d'oeuvres in the parlor in front of a warm fireplace. Luxuriate in Jacuzzi tubs, private baths, and central air. Enjoy English antiques and herb gardens, or relax in our inground pool with decks that overlook the lake. Marvel at spectacular sunsets and vibrant fall colors. Plan to enjoy one of the many local festivals, or just take a romantic walk on a fantastic beach.

Rates at The Chestnut House Bed & Breakfast range from $68-$120.
Rates include a full breakfast.

Sausage and Potato Breakfast Torta

A breakfast favorite at our home; it's scrumptious and easy to prepare. It's not only timesaving but convenient to make the night before. Cover and refrigerate, then bake it in the morning. We usually accompany the torta with spicy cheese grits or fried green tomatoes.

makes one 13x9-inch casserole

1 1/2 pounds hot Italian sausage
1 1/2 pounds frozen hash brown
       potatoes
    2 tablespoons vegetable oil
  1/2 cup chopped green onions
  1/2 cup chopped green pepper
  1/2 cup chopped red pepper

   10 eggs, beaten
  1/2 cup milk
  1/2 teaspoon dry mustard
  1/2 teaspoon black pepper
    1 tube (8 ounces) crescent rolls
2 1/2 cups grated Cheddar cheese
       Dash of paprika

Preheat oven to 350 degrees. Spray a 13x9-inch casserole dish with non-stick cooking spray.

In a large skillet, fry sausage until browned; drain well and set aside. Fry potatoes in oil; add onions and peppers, frying until tender. In a large bowl, combine eggs, milk, mustard, and black pepper. Whisk well and set aside.

Line bottom of prepared dish with crescent roll dough; layer sausage, potatoes, and cheese. Pour egg mixture over top of casserole. Sprinkle with paprika.

Bake 40-45 minutes. Remove from oven and let stand 5 minutes before serving.

South Cliff Inn
Bed and Breakfast

1900 Lakeshore Drive
St. Joseph, MI 49085
616-983-4881

Host: Bill Swisher

*S*outh Cliff Inn is a beautifully renovated bed and breakfast, setting on a bluff overlooking Lake Michigan in the quaint village of Saint Joseph. The exterior of the Inn is brick and much like an English cottage, complete with a formal perennial garden and decks overlooking the lake. South Cliff is finished with custom-designed furnishings and many antiques. Each of the seven beautifully appointed guest rooms has a private bath. A number of rooms have fireplaces, whirlpool tubs or both, and several have balconies overlooking the lake. The atmosphere is one of warmth and friendliness. The innkeeper is a retired chef, so get ready to enjoy the homemade breakfast.

South Cliff Inn has received the Readers Choice Award for the best bed and breakfast in southwestern Michigan in 1994, 1995, and 1996. We strive to make your stay most enjoyable and relaxing.

Rates at South Cliff Inn Bed & Breakfast range from $75-$150.
Rates include brunch on Sunday and a continental-plus breakfast
during the week.

Plum Goodie Coffee Cake

This coffee cake is always a favorite with my guests. It is good served warm or at room temperature. You can substitute many other fruits such as canned or fresh peaches for the plums. Be sure to soften, not melt, the butter when preparing the cake. This will result in a beautiful coffee cake rather than a flat large pancake.

makes one 8-inch coffee cake

1¼ cups plus ⅓ cup flour, divided
¾ cup granulated sugar
2 teaspoons baking powder
½ teaspoon salt
8 tablespoons butter, softened, divided
1 egg, slightly beaten
¼ cup milk
½ teaspoon rum flavoring

6-10 ripe plums
4 tablespoons brown sugar
½ teaspoon cinnamon

Glaze:
1 tablespoon butter, melted
½ cup powdered sugar
3 teaspoons milk (approximately)
½ teaspoon rum flavoring

In a medium bowl, combine 1¼ cups of the flour, granulated sugar, baking powder, salt, and 6 tablespoons of the butter with a pastry blender until crumbly (much like coarse cornmeal).

Mix together egg, milk, and rum flavoring in a separate bowl. Add to flour mixture; stir until just combined.

Prepare an 8- or 9-inch springform pan by spraying with nonstick cooking spray. Spread batter in bottom of pan.

Pit and slice plums. Place over dough, covering entire surface. Combine remaining 2 tablespoons butter, brown sugar, remaining ⅓ cup flour, and cinnamon with pastry blender until crumbly; sprinkle over plums. Bake at 350 degrees for 40-60 minutes, or until a wooden pick inserted in center comes out clean. Remove from oven and let stand 10 minutes before pouring glaze over cake. To make glaze, combine butter, powdered sugar, milk, and rum flavoring in a small bowl; mix till smooth.

The Yellow Rose
Bed & Breakfast

220 East Washington Street
St. Louis, MI 48880
517-681-5296

Hosts: Rich and Di Leonard

*T*he Yellow Rose Bed and Breakfast is located in "the middle of the mitten." Our beautiful three-guest room, antique-furnished 1904 Victorian home awaits your arrival. A rose is gently placed on your bed, and complementary wine and snacks are available upon request. Awake to an elegantly served candlelight breakfast. Then spend the day in area antique shops, on the golf course, or at the casino.

Rates at The Yellow Rose Bed & Breakfast range from $55-$85.
Rates include a full breakfast.

Creamy Delight Yogurt

For those that just aren't sure they care for yogurt, this dish is a must! It's light, creamy, and delicious. Try seasonal fresh berries such as raspberries or huckleberries as a substitute for apples.

serves 6

1 container (32 ounces) Dannon Light Vanilla Yogurt
2 large Granny Smith apples (reserve 6 slices for garnish)
cut into bite-size pieces
1/2 cup light brown sugar
1/2 cup chopped walnuts or pecans (optional)

Spoon yogurt into bottom of stemmed dessert glass; top with apple (layers should be approximately 1/4-inch thick). Continue to layer yogurt and apples to about 3/4-inch from top of glass. Sprinkle with 1/2 teaspoon brown sugar and cover with plastic wrap; refrigerate 30 minutes. Top with a sprinkling of nuts and garnish with apple slice.

Kemah Guest House

633 Allegan Street
Saugatuck, MI 49453
616-857-2919

Host: Daniel Osborn, Innkeeper; Terry and Cindy Tatsch, Owners

The Kemah Guest House is located in the residential section "on the hill" in Saugatuck and looks across the harbor of the Kalamazoo River. It is only three short blocks to the center of town, where shopping, antiquing, great eating (some of the best ice cream in the state), and walking on one of the longest boardwalks in Michigan await you.

Originally a 1906 seaman's cottage, it was transformed into a 6,000-square-foot mansion in 1926 by a local artist/architect from the famous Oxbow Artist's Retreat. A secret cave, a buried Indian, the hidden rathskeller, and remnants of the basement "speakeasy" are delightful additions to the comfortable ambiance of the house.

Opened in 1984, the Kemah features six guest rooms: two with whirlpool tubs and seven rooms of common area. The off-season months of November-April offer weekend entertainment packages with special dining options.

Rates at Kemah Guest House range from $85-$140.
Rates include a very hearty continental breakfast.

Gooey Cinnamon Ring

There just never seems to be enough of this recipe to go around, so I always make twice as much as I think I will need. This popular breakfast item is sure to give everyone a serious wake-up call when baked as guests begin to awaken to the smell. It is especially timesaving when prepared late the night before. Place pan in cold oven; it should be the proper readiness in the morning—just turn on the oven and bake. Serve piping hot. Optional toppings include raisins, nuts, or a small can of fruit pie filling.

makes 1 cinnamon ring

1 loaf frozen bread dough, thawed
1 package (3.4 ounces) cook and serve
     butterscotch pudding
1/2 cup (1 stick) butter or margarine
1 tablespoon cinnamon
3/4 cup brown sugar
     Chopped nuts (optional)
     Raisins (optional)

Spray a Bundt pan with nonstick cooking spray. (Add optional ingredients at this time, if desired.) Cut thawed dough into 4 long strips; then cut each strip into 8 equal pieces. Place strips in pan to evenly cover bottom. Sprinkle dry pudding over top of strips.

Melt butter in a small saucepan. Add cinnamon and brown sugar; stir until well mixed. Pour over dough and pudding. Allow dough to raise to top of pan. Bake in a 325-degree oven for 20-25 minutes. Cool in pan 10 minutes, then invert to serving platter.

The Newnham SunCatcher Inn

131 Griffith Street
PO Box 1106
Saugatuck, MI 49453
616-857-4249

Hosts: Barb Wishon and Nancy Parker

*T*he Newnham home was built circa 1900. Period-style furniture and decorative touches grace its five bedrooms, sitting room, and kitchen. A unique feature of the home is a large sun deck with hot tub and a heated inground swimming pool. Nestled in back of the main house is a quaint and comfortable fully equipped and furnished two-suite cottage with fireplace.

The Newnham SunCatcher Inn is located on a secluded lot in the heart of Saugatuck's business district one block from shops and restaurants and just minutes from Lake Michigan beaches and recreational facilities.

A full breakfast is served from 9:30-10:30 a.m. in the dining room or poolside.

Rates at The Newnham SunCatcher Inn range from $65-$120.
Rates include a full breakfast.

Toasted Almond Sticky Buns

*The smell of fresh-baked bread and the gooey goodness of caramel will convince
your guests that you've spent the morning in the kitchen. It just isn't so with
this easy recipe. It starts with prepared refrigerator dough and ends with
"oohs" and "aahs" from guests. This recipe can easily be cut in half, but I usually make 12 so "seconds" can be sent along with guests as they depart.*

makes 12 sweet rolls

1/2 cup firmly packed brown sugar

2 teaspoons flour

2 tablespoons margarine,
     softened

1 tablespoon milk

1/2 teaspoon almond extract

2 tubes (8 ounces each) crescent
     roll dough

Filling:

1 tablespoon margarine, melted

1/8 teaspoon almond extract

1/4 cup toasted chopped almonds

Glaze:

1/2 cup powdered sugar

2-3 teaspoons milk

1/8 teaspoon almond extract

In a small bowl, combine sugar, flour, margarine, milk, and almond
extract; blend well. Spoon mixture into 12 ungreased muffin cups.

Separate crescent roll dough into 4 rectangles; firm, pressing perforations
to seal seams.

To make filling, combine margarine and almond extract; blend well. Brush
over each rectangle; sprinkle with almonds. Starting at short side, roll up jelly
roll fashion; pinch seams to seal. Cut each roll into 3 slices. Place cut side
down in muffin cups.

Bake at 375 degrees for 15-20 minutes, or until golden brown.
Immediately invert onto wire rack.

To prepare glaze, combine powdered sugar, milk, and almond extract in a
small bowl. Drizzle glaze over warm sticky buns.

The Park House
Bed & Breakfast

888 Holland
Saugatuck, MI 49453
616-857-4535
Hosts: Lynda and Joe Petty

Welcome to The Park House...come stay with us and relive a bit of Saugatuck history. Built in 1857 by lumberman H. D. Moore, The Park House is Saugatuck's oldest residence. From Susan B. Anthony to the early Oxbow artists, guests of The Park House have enjoyed cordial atmosphere and winsome surroundings.

Eight bedrooms with queen-sized beds and private baths offer the charm of brass and seasoned woods. Snuggle by the fireplaces or hide away in a Jacuzzi suite, where breakfast is served on your private balcony. For ultimate privacy, cottages are available. Join us fireside in the commons room or gardenside on the screened porch for a buffet breakfast. A short walk will take you to the heart of Saugatuck shopping on the banks of the Kalamazoo River. And just beyond the dunes, Lake Michigan calls.

Open year-round, guests can enjoy Michigan's winter vista, candlelit Christmas, and invigorating cross-country ski weekends.

Rates at The Park House Bed & Breakfast range from $85-$150.
Rates include a full breakfast.

Fresh Salsa

There are many wonderful recipes for salsa, but this is our absolute favorite.
It tastes so fresh and it has zip and crunch. Enjoy it with tortilla chips
while relaxing in the sun.

makes 4 cups

6 roma tomatoes, chopped
1 small onion, chopped
1/2 small head cabbage, chopped
1-2 sarona peppers, finely chopped
1/2 teaspoon garlic salt

Combine tomatoes, onion, cabbage, peppers, and garlic salt in a medium bowl; blend until well mixed. Refrigerate until serving.

Wickwood Country Inn

510 Butler Street
PO Box 1019
Saugatuck, MI 49453
616-857-1465

Hosts: Bill and Julee Rosso Miller

This truly elegant and stately Inn is in the resort village of Saugatuck located on a beautiful yachting harbor leading to Lake Michigan. The Inn is filled with French and English antiques, Oriental rugs, overstuffed chairs, vases of flowers, candlelight, a library of fine books, music, and original drawings and oils. Each guest room is decorated using a unique seasonal, country, or historical theme. A generous breakfast buffet starts the day, and tasty hors d'oeuvres are served each evening.

Privacy and comfort are the key words—with lots of activity just outside its doors.

Rates at Wickwood Country Inn range from $125-$195.
Rates include a brunch on weekends and a continental buffet
breakfast during the week.

The Wickwood Summer Tart with Red Pepper Pesto

Everyone seems to love this tart. I think it's probably because it really has the taste of summer, but it can be made anytime of the year. Red Pepper Pesto will keep for one week in the refrigerator.

serves 12 as a luncheon entree or 24 as an appetizer

Red Pepper Pesto:
- 3 medium red peppers
- 1 tablespoon lemon juice
- 1/8 teaspoon cayenne pepper
- 1 plump garlic clove, minced
- 1/2 tablespoon olive oil
- 1 1/2 tablespoons sugar

Tart:
- 2 sheets (9x9 inches each) puff pastry, thawed
- 1 1/2 cups shredded mozzarella
- 10 ripe roma tomatoes, sliced 1/4-inch thick
- 1 1/2 cups shredded Parmesan cheese
- 1/4 cup finely minced basil
- 1 cup Parmesan curls*

Wash peppers; slice in half horizontally. Remove stem, membrane, and seeds. Make 1/4-inch vertical slits, approximately 1 inch apart, around bottom of pepper and flatten each half with hand.

Position oven rack about 4 inches from boiler. Arrange peppers skin side up on baking sheet and broil until completely blackened. Remove and place peppers in a container, seal, and steam 15-20 minutes. When cool, remove skin.

In a blender or food processor, puree peppers. Add lemon juice, cayenne, garlic, and oil. Add sugar 1 tablespoon at a time or to taste. Blend till smooth.

Preheat oven to 375 degrees. Roll pastry sheets to fit a 15 1/2x10 1/2x1-inch jelly roll pan. Cut and piece pastry onto bottom and up sides of baking sheet, covering sides to the height of the edge or higher. Use water to seal seams, if necessary. Spread 1/2 cup pesto evenly over pastry. (Refrigerate or freeze remaining pesto.) Sprinkle mozzarella over pesto; arrange tomato slices in rows over cheese. Top with Parmesan and basil. Scatter Parmesan curls over entire pan. Bake 45 minutes or until golden brown. Serve immediately.

*Note: A potato peeler can be used to make Parmesan curls.

A Country Place
Bed & Breakfast

79 North Shore Drive North
South Haven, MI 49090
616-637-5523

Hosts: Art and Lee Niffenegger

Warm, gracious hospitality awaits your arrival including a greeting from our friendly resident cat, Munchie. We provide personal orientation and direct you to fine restaurants, quaint shops, and championship golf courses. A Lake Michigan beach access is only steps away.

The English country theme throughout our restored 1860s Greek Revival is created by lovely florals and antique treasures collected while living in England. A leisurely "sin"sational full breakfast is served by the fireside or on the spacious deck.

A tea cart and refrigerator is stocked with complementary drinks, snacks, and homemade delicacies. Other luxuries include top-quality beds/linens and goose down duvets in each of our five guest rooms.

Rates at A Country Place Bed & Breakfast range from $70-$95.
Rates include a full breakfast.

Southwest Casserole

It took a long time to get the courage to serve this recipe for breakfast.
Old and young alike love it and plates always return empty. I make this for
the next day right after breakfast is served.

serves 6-8

4 ounces Cheddar cheese, grated (1 cup)
4 ounces jalapeno jack cheese, grated (1 cup)
4 eggs
1 cup cottage cheese
1 cup packaged biscuit mix
2 cups milk
1/2 teaspoon dried cilantro
1/2 teaspoon cumin
Salsa
Fresh cilantro

Spray an 11x7x2-inch casserole with nonstick cooking spray. Spread cheeses evenly over bottom.

In a large bowl, whisk eggs. Add cottage cheese, biscuit mix, and 1 cup of the milk. Mix until well blended. Add remaining 1 cup milk. (Mixture will be thin and lumpy.) Pour over cheeses. Cover casserole and place in refrigerator overnight.

Preheat oven to 350 degrees. Before baking, uncover casserole and sprinkle with cilantro and cumin. Bake about 45 minutes, or until a knife inserted in center comes out clean. Let stand 10 minutes before cutting and serving. Serve with a side of salsa and cilantro sprig on each piece.

The Seymour House
Bed & Breakfast

1248 Blue Star Highway
South Haven, MI 49090
616-227-3918

Hosts: Tom and Gwen Paton

*T*he Seymour House is a stately brick Italianate-style Victorian mansion with original pocket doors and intricate carved wood trim on doors and windows. Enjoy nature and ultimate relaxation on 11 picturesque acres with maintained nature trails, a stocked one-acre pond, and garden patio. A beautifully presented gourmet breakfast awaits you each morning. This Inn has five guest rooms (several include fireplaces) and private baths (some with Jacuzzis). A guest log cabin is available for a more rustic experience. The Inn is minutes away from the popular resort towns of Saugatuck and South Haven and is one-half mile from Lake Michigan.

Treat yourself—come and enjoy this picturesque setting.

Rates at The Seymour House Bed & Breakfast range from $75-$129.
Rates include a gourmet full breakfast.

Popovers

Watch people ooh and aah as you bring these popovers to the table! They are individually shaped as they come from the oven and must be served steaming hot! Popovers are very gourmet, yet require few ingredients. I like to make extras in case some stick in the pan. We also pass a shaker of cinnamon and sugar so guests may sprinkle the mixture right on top of their hot popover.

makes 8 popovers

2 eggs
1 cup whole milk
1 cup flour
1/2 teaspoon salt

Topping (optional):
1/4 teaspoon cinnamon
1/4 cup sugar

Preheat oven to 450 degrees. Grease muffin cups and top surface of tin with shortening.

Beat eggs in a medium bowl; add milk, flour, and salt all at once. Beat only until blended. (Batter will appear lumpy.) Pour into 8 prepared muffin cups and bake 15 minutes at 450 degrees, then lower temperature to 350 degrees and bake another 15 minutes.

Serve immediately with butter and cinnamon-sugar topping.

Yelton Manor
Bed & Breakfast

140 North Shore Drive
South Haven, MI 49090
616-637-5220

Hosts: Elaine Herbert and Rob Kripaitis

The Yelton Manor Bed and Breakfast is two magnificent three-story Victorian mansions overlooking the Lake Michigan shoreline. Surrounded by extensive gardens and tended by pampering innkeepers, The Manor has been named among the top ten B&Bs in the USA by Amoco Motor Club.

The Manor has porches, parlors, extensive book and video libraries, music, art collections, lovely antiques, and elegant decor. All 17 rooms have private baths and TV/VCRs. Most have a Jacuzzi and fireplace, while some have balconies and lovely lake views.

When you are at Yelton Manor Bed & Breakfast, you will under-stand why the *Chicago Sun Times* named it "Top of the Crop in Luxury B&B's!"

Rates at Yelton Manor Bed and Breakfast range from $90-$220.
Rates include a full breakfast.

Salsa Elaine

This wonderfully spicy tomato salsa is served fresh from July through October at The Manor for breakfast, as an hors d'oeuvre, recipe ingredient, or a spoonable relish. We've been known to put up over 500 jars, so we have it all winter too! The food processor helps make it easier, and there's nothing like the pure taste of an August harvest on a February table. Process jars in a water bath or pressure cooker using proper canning methods and cooking times. Use rubber gloves when removing seeds from jalapeno peppers, being extremely careful not to touch skin or eyes during handling.

makes 7 quarts

25-35	perfect ripe tomatoes
12	bunches scallions, chopped
12-20	fresh jalapeno peppers, seeded and sliced
10	cloves garlic, peeled
12	bunches fresh cilantro

Fill a large kettle with water; bring to a boil. Carefully lower tomatoes into boiling water; boil 1-2 minutes, or until skins burst. Using a slotted spoon, lift tomatoes from kettle and slip off skins. Chop tomatoes and put in a large bowl. (Use a baster to syphon liquid from bowl as tomatoes drain.) Add scallions.

Place peppers and garlic in a food processor; chop until fine; set aside. Chop cilantro with a large chef's knife—enjoy the delightfully pungent aroma! Combine tomatoes, scallions, peppers, garlic, and cilantro; mix until well blended.

Salsa will keep in the refrigerator 4-5 days. If making fresh salsa each week, divide in half; serve one and preserve remainder to ensure all-season availability.

The Royal Pontaluna Inn

1870 Pontaluna Road
Spring Lake, MI 49456
616-798-7271 or 800-865-3545

Hosts: Charles and Di Beacham

The Royal Pontaluna Inn is situated on 27 acres of park-like grounds just minutes from Lake Michigan. Our unique, contemporary Inn is more like a mini-resort with a large indoor pool, sauna, whirlpool, and tennis court. The five guest rooms are individually decorated and air-conditioned. All include queen-size beds, private baths (most with Jacuzzis), TV, and VCR. A special feature of the Inn is the "Royal Suite," a romantic haven with a fireplace and two-person Jacuzzi. Open year-round, we invite you to make yourselves at home by enjoying a stroll through the hardwoods and scattering pines, relaxing in front of the fireplace with your favorite book, or sitting on the deck appreciating the flower gardens and wildlife which surrounds the Inn.

Rates at The Royal Pontaluna Inn Bed & Breakfast range from $85-$139.
Rates include a full breakfast.

Chocolate Chip (Egg-Free) Cookies

*As its name states, this recipe does not require the use of eggs.
The cookies turn out very tender and freeze extremely well.*

makes 2-3 dozen cookies

1 cup (2 sticks) butter or butter-flavored Crisco
1 teaspoon vanilla extract
1 cup powdered sugar
1 1/2 cups flour
1/2 teaspoon baking soda
1 cup quick-cooking oats
1 cup semisweet chocolate chips

Preheat oven to 350 degrees.

Cream together butter, vanilla, and powdered sugar in a large bowl. In a separate bowl, combine flour, baking soda, and oats; stir into creamed mixture. (Mixture may be slightly dry—do not add liquid.) Mix in chocolate chips; stir to combine.

Drop rounded tablespoons of dough, 2 inches apart, onto ungreased cookie sheet. Bake 8-10 minutes, or until golden brown. Cool cookies on baking sheet; carefully remove and store in an airtight container.

Seascape Bed & Breakfast

20009 Breton
Spring Lake, MI 49456
616-842-8409

Hostess: Susan Meyer

Seascape Bed & Breakfast is located on a private sandy Lake Michigan beach with relaxing lakefront rooms. Enjoy the warm hospitality and "country living" ambiance of our nautical lakeshore home. A full homemade breakfast is served in either the gathering room (with fieldstone fireplace), glassed-in porch, or large open deck. All rooms offer panoramic views of Lake Michigan and Grand Haven Harbor.

Stroll in this quiet setting or cross-country ski through duneland preserve. Open year-round, Seascape Bed & Breakfast offers a kaleidoscope of scenes with the changing of the seasons. A romantic Victorian cottage, which sleeps eight, is also available for private retreats.

Rates at Seascape Bed & Breakfast range from $85-$150.
Rates include a full breakfast.

Spinach Breakfast Pie

I combine the first five ingredients (ham, cheeses, onion, and spinach) the day before, cover with plastic wrap, and refrigerate in a quiche pan overnight. This saves time and cleanup in the morning. Since this dish is cooked in the microwave (only 17 minutes), the morning is never rushed! This dish is appealing to the eye and pleasing to the palate. I like to serve it on glass plates with homemade muffins and a fresh fruit compote.

serves 8

1 cup diced ham	1 cup milk
3/4 cup shredded Swiss cheese	1 1/4 cups firmly packed Bisquick
3/4 cup shredded Cheddar cheese	4 large eggs
2/3 cup diced onion	1/4 teaspoon salt
1/2 package (5 ounces) frozen spinach, moisture removed	1/4 teaspoon pepper

Combine ham, cheeses, and onion in a medium bowl. Add spinach; mix well. Spread mixture evenly over bottom of lightly greased quiche pan or 9-inch pie plate.

In a large bowl, combine milk, Bisquick, eggs, salt, and pepper. Beat with electric mixer on high speed 1 minute. Pour evenly over ham and cheese mixture.

Microwave uncovered on high for 17 minutes. Let stand 5 minutes; cut in 8 pie-shaped pieces when ready to serve.

Open Windows
Bed & Breakfast

613 St. Mary's Avenue
PO Box 698
Suttons Bay, MI 49682
616-271-4300 or 800-520-3722

Hosts: Don and Norma Blumenschine

*O*pen Windows Bed & Breakfast is a charming century-old farmhouse, complete with gardens and picket fences, located in the village of Suttons Bay on the Leelanau Peninsula, 15 miles north of Traverse City. The village, beaches, marina, shops, and fine restaurants are just a short walk away.

Our home, beautifully decorated with your comfort in mind, has three bedrooms with private baths for guests. The front porch, deck, lounge, fireplace, and our warm hospitality offer you the opportunity to unwind, relax, and enjoy your visit to the fullest.

Breakfast is always a special event with everything plentiful and homemade. We feature wonderful fruits available from local growers.

Rates at Open Windows Bed & Breakfast range from $90-$105.
Rates include a full breakfast.

Honeydew Cherry Salad

An elegant beginning to breakfast, this salad is a gentle blend of flavors that appeals to almost everyone. It is a favorite first course at Open Windows. Along with many other orchard fruits, the Leelanau Peninsula produces nearly one million pounds of cherries a year. Therefore dried tart cherries are featured in many of our recipes. We often substitute cherries in recipes calling for raisins. In the Honeydew Cherry Salad, fat-free regular or low-fat sour cream can be used as a substitute for sour cream.

serves 6-8

3-4 cups honeydew melon balls
1/4 cup chopped pecans or walnuts
1/4 cup coconut flakes
1/2 cup dried tart cherries
8 ounces sour cream
2 tablespoons apricot preserves

In a medium bowl, gently mix melon balls, nuts, coconut, and cherries. Refrigerate until serving time. Just before serving, mix together sour cream and apricot preserves. Fold into fruit mixture. Spoon salad into individual parfait glasses and garnish with a slice of lime or orange, if desired.

Victoriana 1898

622 Washington Street
Traverse City, MI 49686
616-929-1009

Hosts: Flo and Bob Schermerhorn

Victoriana 1898 is nestled on a tree-lined street in an area filled with Victorian homes. It's only a short walk from one of Michigan's best downtown shopping districts and the beach; local wineries, museums, galleries, and sand dunes are just a pleasant drive away. The Innkeepers are longtime antique collectors and have combined their collection with traditional furnishings and rich Persian carpets. Warm brown gingerbread trim, old oak, and family heirlooms accent the home's interior. The Innkeepers are always glad to share the Inn's rich history with guests. Breakfast entrees range from stuffed French toast or waffles with strawberry-rhubarb sauce to creative quiches.

Rates at Victoriana 1898 range from $60-$85.
Rates include a full breakfast.

Crab Scramble

*This recipe was given to us from our friend Lois who lives out East.
It adds a nice elegance to a breakfast menu and tastes
marvelous too.*

serves 6

1/2 cup (1 stick) butter
9 eggs, slightly beaten
1/2 cup milk
1 package (8 ounces) cream cheese, cubed
1 can (6 ounces) crabmeat, flaked
1/2 teaspoon salt
1/4 teaspoon pepper
1 tablespoon chopped fresh dill
Fresh fruit for garnish

Melt butter in a 12x7-inch pan. In a medium bowl, add eggs, milk, cream cheese, crabmeat, salt, and pepper; pour into pan over butter. Bake at 350 degrees for 30 minutes. Remove from oven and let rest 5 minutes. To serve, cut into squares and sprinkle with dill.

Garden Grove
Bed & Breakfast

9549 Union Pier Road
Union Pier, MI 49129
616-469-6346

Hosts: Ric and Mary Ellen Postlewaite

Nestled in the countryside of Union Pier (a charming resort community along the shores of Lake Michigan) lies a romantic retreat, a reminder of a time past when the world moved slower. Garden Grove is everything the discriminating Inn guest has come to expect: charm, beauty, a scrumptious breakfast, and an outstanding location.

Set in a vintage 1925 cottage-style home, Garden Grove has been lovingly renovated and whimsically decorated with vibrant colors and botanical influences to bring the garden indoors year-round. The Inn features fireplaces, whirlpool tubs, original wood floors throughout, and garden views from every window. There is a fireplace in the parlor, an extensive library (both books and videos), games, and snacks. Mountain bikes are also available for touring the countryside.

Breakfasts are not to be missed, served at individual dining tables on a colorful collection of china. No detail is too small.

Rates at Garden Grove Bed & Breakfast range from $80-$150.
Rates include a full breakfast.

Potato Pancakes

We created this recipe to serve to a family having a reunion at our Inn. They were all very concerned about fat and cholesterol in their diets and were delighted by this modern version of an old favorite. The cool applesauce and sour cream mellow the bite of the pepper and onion.

makes 12 pancakes

1 bag (26 ounces) frozen shredded potatoes, thawed
    overnight
2 tablespoons flour
2 teaspoons salt
1 teaspoon coarsely ground black pepper
1/2 teaspoon thyme
1 carton (8 ounces) Egg Beaters
4 tablespoons corn oil
3 green onions, finely chopped

In a large bowl, mix together potatoes, flour, 2 teaspoons salt or to taste, pepper, thyme, Egg Beaters, oil, and onions. Spoon mixture onto hot griddle and spread into 1/4-inch-thick pancakes. Cook about 8 minutes on each side, or until pancakes are brown and crispy. Pancakes can be lightly cooked and held in a warm oven, then returned to a hot griddle and finished later.

Serve with applesauce and nonfat sour cream on the side.

White Swan Inn

303 South Mears Avenue
Whitehall, MI 49461
616-894-5169 or 888 WHT SWAN (948-7926)

Hosts: Cathy and Ron Russell

*B*uilt in 1884 for a sawmill owner, the White Swan Inn is a Queen Anne-style home located in the wonderful resort area of White Lake. Spacious bedrooms with private baths, a large screened porch with white wicker furniture, and a beautiful inlaid parquet floor highlighting the dining room are just a few of the delights at the White Swan Inn.

Every season offers a variety of outdoor activities such as theater, concerts, and museums. Walk to shops, dining, and White Lake, or use our bikes for a trip on the nearby Hart-Montague Trail. For a great get-away, visit the White Swan Inn.

Rates at White Swan Inn start from $67.
Rates include a full breakfast.

Ham and Cheese Crescent

This recipe makes a delicious breakfast/brunch entree. With the addition of a green salad, you have a quick and filling dinner. Lowered fat and fat-free ingredients can be selected with equally pleasing results.

serves 2-3

1 tube (8 ounces) crescent roll dough
2 tablespoons honey mustard
1/4 pound smoked ham or turkey ham, chopped
1/2 cup broccoli flowerets, small pieces (lightly steamed, if desired)
2 ounces Cheddar cheese, shredded
3-4 orange slices, cut and twist for garnish

Unroll dough onto ungreased baking sheet; pinch perforations together. Spread mustard lengthwise down center third of dough. Place ham and broccoli on top of mustard; top with cheese.

With a sharp knife make diagonal cuts to each side of dough (approximately 1 1/2 inches apart). Crisscross dough over ham and cheese filling, sealing ends by pinching dough together.

Bake in a preheated 350-degree oven 16 minutes, or until golden brown. Transfer to a serving platter. Garnish with orange twists and serve.

The Parish House Inn

103 South Huron Street
Ypsilanti, MI 48197
313-480-4800 or 800-480-4866

Hostess: Mrs. Chris Mason

*O*riginally the parsonage for the First Congregational Church, this 1893 Queen Anne-style house has been totally restored to its original Victorian elegance. There are nine guest rooms available, all with the modern amenities. Located in the Historic District, it is within easy walking distance of restaurants, parks, and shopping. Eastern Michigan University, the University of Michigan, golf courses, antique shops, and historical sites are just minutes away.

A "bottomless" cookie jar, popcorn, and soft juices await your arrival. A large video library is also available for your enjoyment.

The aroma of freshly-brewed coffee will be your wake-up call to a hearty breakfast of quiche, pancakes or waffles, scones, and more. Special-occasion packages are also available from The Parish House Inn.

Rates at The Parish House Inn range from $60-$115.
Rates include a full breakfast.

Michigan Baked Oatmeal

Baked in the oven, this oatmeal casserole has a pudding-like consistency. Guests can smell it baking long before they reach the breakfast table—and are often surprised to find out the fresh cookie smell is oatmeal! They are never surprised by the flavor—it tastes as good as it smells.
Vary the optional ingredients to your own liking, using what is on hand in your cupboards. One favorite variation at The Parish House is to omit the almonds, almond flavoring, and cherries. Instead add 1 tablespoon cinnamon, 1/2 cup raisins, and 1/2 cup peanuts, chopped.

serves 6-8

2 cups old-fashioned rolled oats
4 cups milk
1/2 teaspoon almond flavoring
1/4 cup brown sugar
1/2 cup sliced almonds
1/2 cup dried cherries
1 large apple, unpeeled and grated

Preheat oven to 400 degrees. Coat a 3-quart casserole or baking pan with nonstick cooking spray.

In a large bowl, combine oats, milk, almond flavoring, sugar, almonds, cherries, and apple. Transfer to baking dish. Sprinkle top with additional almonds.

Bake uncovered 45 minutes. Serve hot.

Directory of the Michigan Lake to Lake Bed & Breakfast Association

Directory of the
Michigan Lake to Lake Bed & Breakfast Association

Bold type: For more information on this Inn, see the page listed.

CITY	INN/PHONE
Adrian	Briaroaks Inn 517-263-1659
Alden	Torch Lake B&B 616-331-6424
Algonac	Linda's Lighthouse Inn 810-794-2992
Allegan	**Castle in the Country Bed & Breakfast 616-673-8054**
	Cinnamon Sensation Coffee Cake, page 9
	Winchester Inn B&B 616-673-3621
Alma	**Saravilla Bed & Breakfast 517-463-4078**
	Friendship Granola, page 11
Ann Arbor	The Artful Lodger 313-769-0653
	The Urban Retreat 313-971-8110
	Pear-Sausage Soufflé, page 13
Atlanta	**The Briley Inn 517-785-4784**
	Ginger Pancakes with Fresh Peach Topping, page 15
Au Train	Au Train Lake Bed & Breakfast 906-892-8892
	Pinewood Lodge 906-892-8300
Bad Axe	Gray Stone Manor 517-269-9466
Battle Creek	Greencrest Manor 616-962-8633
	The Old Lamplighters Bed & Breakfast 616-963-2603
Bay City	Clements Inn 517-894-4600
Bay View	The Florence 616-348-3322
	The Gingerbread House 616-347-3538
Bellaire	Bellaire Bed & Breakfast 616-533-6077
	Grand Victorian Bed & Breakfast Inn 616-533-6111
Beulah	The Windermere Inn 616-882-9000
Big Bay	**Big Bay Point Lighthouse Bed & Breakfast 906-345-9957**
	Cheese Blintzes, page 17
Birch Run	Church Street Manor 517-624-4920
Blissfield	Hiram D. Ellis Inn 517-486-3155
Boyne City	The Beardsley House 616-582-9619
	Deer Lake Bed & Breakfast 616-582-9039
	Duley's State Street Inn 616-582-7855
Bridgeport	Karen's House Bed & Breakfast 517-777-7446

CITY	INN/PHONE

Brooklyn
The Chicago Street Inn 517-592-3888
Potato Delight, page 19
Dewey Lake Manor Bed & Breakfast 517-467-7122
Waffles by Joe, page 21

Buchanan
The Primrose Path Bed & Breakfast 616-695-6321

Cadillac
American Inn Bed & Breakfast 616-779-9000
Hoxeyville Hills Bed & Breakfast 616-862-3628
Sausage and Apple Quiche, page 23

Calumet
Holly Manor 906-337-3336

Canton
Willow Brook Inn Bed & Breakfast 313-454-0019
Harvest Pancakes, page 25

Caro
Garden Gate B&B 517-673-2696

Cedarville
Les Cheneaux B&B 906-484-2007

Central Lake
Bridgewalk Bed & Breakfast 616-544-8122
Apple Sausage Blossoms, page 27
Coulter Creek Bed & Breakfast 616-544-3931
Make Ahead Eggs Benedict, page 29

Charlevoix
Aaron's Windy Hill Guest Lodge 616-547-2804
Belvedere Inn 616-547-2251
Buttermilk Cinnamon Bread, page 31
The Bridge Street Inn 616-547-6606
Caine Cottage 616-547-6781
Pineapple Breakfast Bread, page 33
Charlevoix Country Inn 616-547-5134
MacDougall House B&B 616-547-5788
The Tall Ship "Appledore" 616-547-0024

Charlotte
Schatze Manor Bed & Breakfast 517-543-4170

Chesaning
Stone House B&B 517-845-4440

Clarkston
Millpond Inn 810-620-6520

Clio
The Cinnamon Stick Farm Bed & Breakfast 810-686-8391
Country-Style Potato and Onion Pie, page 35

Coldwater
Chicago Pike Inn 517-279-8744
Curried Fruit Bake, page 37

Colon
Palmer Lake Bed & Breakfast 616-432-4498

Constantine
Our Olde House Bed & Breakfast Inn 616-435-3325

Dearborn
Dearborn Bed & Breakfast 313-563-2200

Douglas
Goshorn House 616-857-1326

CITY	INN/PHONE

Douglas
(cont.)

The Kirby House 616-857-2904
    Shaker Cheese Squares, page 39
Sherwood Forest B&B 616-857-1246

Dundee   The Dundee Guest House 313-529-5706

East Jordan   Easterly Inn 616-536-3434

East Tawas   **East Tawas Junction Bed & Breakfast 517-362-8006**
    Eggs en Cocotte Lorraine, page 41

Eastport   Torch Lake Sunrise Bed & Breakfast 616-599-2706

Elk Rapids   Cairn House Bed & Breakfast 616-264-8994
Candlelight Inn 616-264-5630

Ellsworth   Ellsworth House 616-588-7001
A House on the Hill 616-588-6304
Lake Michigan's Abiding Place 616-599-2808

Empire   South Bar Manor 616-326-5304

Farmington Hills   Locust Manor Bed & Breakfast 810-471-2278

Fennville   Hidden Pond 616-561-2491
The Kingsley House Bed & Breakfast 616-561-6425
    Honey-Glazed Pecan French Toast, page 43

Frankenmuth   **Bavarian Town Bed & Breakfast 517-652-8057**
    Bavarian Ham Strata, page 45
Bed & Breakfast at The Pines 517-652-9019
Franklin Haus 517-652-3939

Frankfort   **The Birch Haven Inn 616-352-4008**
    Birch Haven Eggs, page 47
Frankfort Land Company 616-352-9267

Fruitport   **Village Park Bed & Breakfast 616-865-6289**
    Country Potato Jubilee, page 49

Galien   The Valentine House 616-756-2223

Garden   The Summer House Bed & Breakfast 906-644-2457

Gladstone   Cartwright's Birdseye Inn 906-428-3997

Glen Arbor   The Sylvan Inn 616-334-4333
White Gull Inn 616-334-4486

Glenn   **Will O'Glenn Irish Bed & Breakfast 616-227-3045**
    Irish Brown Bread, page 51

Grand Haven   Boyden House Inn Bed & Breakfast 616-846-3538
Highland Park Hotel Bed & Breakfast 616-846-1473
    Baked Eggs, page 53

CITY	INN/PHONE
Grand Haven (cont.)	**Lakeshore Bed & Breakfast 616-844-2697**
	Eggs Poached in White Wine, page 55
	Seascape Bed & Breakfast 616-842-8409
	Spinach Breakfast Pie, page 121
Grand Rapids	Fountain Hill Bed & Breakfast 616-458-6621
	Heald-Lear House 616-451-4849
Grass Lake	**Coppy's Inn 517-522-4850**
	Stuffed French Toast with Apple Syrup, page 57
Grayling	**The Hanson House 517-348-6630**
	Blueberry French Toast Cobbler, page 59
Greenville	The Gibson House Bed & Breakfast 616-754-6691
Harbor Springs	Kimberly Country Estate 616-526-7646
	Veranda at Harbor Springs 616-526-7782
	Windy Ridge Bed & Breakfast 616-526-7650
Harrison	Carriage House Inn 517-539-1300
Harrisville	Stratton's Springport Inn Bed & Breakfast 517-724-6308
Hartland	Farmstead Bed & Breakfast Ltd. 810-887-6086
Hillsdale	Bluebird Trails Bed & Breakfast 517-254-4754
Holland	Bonnie's Parsonage 1908 616-396-1316
	Centennial Inn Bed & Breakfast 616-355-0998
	Dutch Colonial Inn 616-396-3664
	North Shore Inn of Holland 616-394-9050
	The Thistle Inn 616-399-0409
	Thistle Inn Crepes, page 61
Holly	**Holly Crossing Bed & Breakfast 810-634-7075**
	Breakfast Casserole, page 63
Houghton	**Charleston House Historic Inn 800-482-7404**
	Finnish Pancake with Raspberry Sauce, page 65
Houghton Lake	Stevens' White House on the Lake 517-366-4567
Hudson	Sutton's Weed Farm Bed & Breakfast 517-547-6302
Interlochen	Between the Lakes B&B 616-276-7751
	Interlochen Aire 616-276-6941
	Sandy Shores Bed & Breakfast 616-276-9763
Ionia	**Union Hill Inn Bed & Breakfast 616-527-0955**
	Asparagus Ham Quiche, page 67
Ithaca	**Bon Accord Farm Bed & Breakfast 517-875-3136**
	Tomato-Basil Frittata, page 69

CITY	INN/PHONE
Jackson	Rose Trellis Bed & Breakfast 517-787-2035
Jones	Sanctuary at Wildwood 616-244-5910
Jonesville	Horse & Carriage B&B 517-849-2732
	The Munro House Bed & Breakfast 517-849-9292
	Orange-Vanilla French Toast, page 71
Kalamazoo	**Hall House Bed & Breakfast 616-343-2500**
	Quick Blueberry Cobbler, page 73
	Stuart Avenue Inn 800-461-0621
	Classic Cream Scones, page 75
Karlin	Hall Creek Bed & Breakfast 616-263-2560
Kearsarge	**Belknap's Garnet House 906-337-5607**
	Zucchini and Mushroom Frittata, page 77
Lake City	Bed & Breakfast in the Pines 616-839-4876
Lake Leelanau	Centennial Inn 616-271-6460
Lake Orion	The Indianwood 810-693-2257
Lakeside	The Pebble House 616-469-1416
	The White Rabbit Inn 616-469-4620
Lansing	Ask Me House 517-484-3127
	Maplewood Bed & Breakfast 517-372-7775
Laurium	**Laurium Manor Inn 906-337-2549**
	Glazed Poppy Seed Muffins, page 79
	Victorian Hall Bed & Breakfast 906-337-2549
Leland	The Aspen House 616-256-9724
	The Highlands of Leland 616-256-7632
	Manitou Manor Bed & Breakfast 616-256-7712
	Snowbird Inn 616-256-9773
Lewiston	Gorton House Bed & Breakfast Inn 517-786-2764
Lexington	Governor's Inn Bed & Breakfast 810-359-5770
	The Powell House B&B 810-359-5533
Lowell	Alden Pines Bed & Breakfast 616-897-5655
	McGee Homestead Bed & Breakfast 616-897-8142
Ludington	Bed & Breakfast at Ludington 616-843-9768
	Doll House Inn 800-275-4616
	Inland Sea B&B 616-845-7569
	The Inn at Ludington 616-845-7055
	The Lamplighter Bed & Breakfast 616-843-9792
	Granola Waffles, page 81
	The Ludington House 616-845-7769

CITY	INN/PHONE
Mackinac Island	Bay View at Mackinac 906-847-3295
	Cloghaun 906-847-3885
	Haan's 1830 Inn 906-847-6244
	Metivier Inn 906-847-6234
Manistee	E. E. Douville House B&B 616-723-8654
	Inn Wick-A-Te-Wah 616-889-4396
	Lake Shore Bed & Breakfast 616-723-7644
	Manistee Country House 616-723-2367
	The Maples 616-723-2904
Marine City	The Heather House 810-765-3175
Marlette	Country View B&B 517-635-2468
Marquette	The Bayou Place 906-249-3863
	Blueberry Ridge B&B 906-249-9246
Marshall	**The National House Inn 616-781-7374**
	Sam Hill Sour Cream Cake, page 83
Mears	The Dunes Bed & Breakfast 616-873-5128
Mendon	The Mendon Country Inn 616-496-8132
Michigamme	Cottage-on-the-Bay Bed & Breakfast 906-323-6191
Midland	The Bramble House B&B 517-832-5082
Muskegon	A Blue Country Bed & Breakfast 616-744-2555
	Emery House Bed & Breakfast 616-722-6978
	Hackley-Holt House 616-725-7303
	Swedish Pancakes, page 85
	Port City Victorian Inn 616-759-0205
	Baked Eggs in Basil Sauce, page 87
New Buffalo	Michigan Lake to Lake B&B Association 616-756-3445
	Sans Souci B&B 616-756-3141
	Tall Oaks Inn 800-936-0034
Newberry	The MacLeod House 906-293-3841
Northport	North Shore Inn 616-386-7111
Omena	Frieda's B&B 616-386-7274
	Omena Shores Bed & Breakfast 616-386-7313
	Omena Sunset Lodge Bed & Breakfast 616-386-9080
Onekama	Lake Breeze House 616-889-4969
Ontonagon	Northern Light Inn 906-884-4290
Oscoda	Huron House Bed & Breakfast 517-739-9255
Owosso	Mulberry House Bed & Breakfast 517-723-4890

CITY	INN/PHONE

Pentwater — **The Candlewyck House Bed & Breakfast 616-869-5967**
  Seafood Quiche, page 89
The Hexagon House 616-869-4102
Historic Nickerson Inn 616-869-6731
The Pentwater Abbey Bed & Breakfast 616-869-4094
The Pentwater Inn 616-869-5909
  Oatmeal Cranberry Scones, page 91

Petoskey — 510 Elizabeth 616-348-3830
Bear River Valley Bed & Breakfast 616-348-2046
  Maple Pecan Granola, page 93
The Cozy Spot 616-347-3869
Montgomery Place Bed & Breakfast 616-347-1338
  Breakfast Sausage Squares, page 95
Serenity—A Bed & Breakfast 616-347-6171
  Orange Scones, page 97

Pinckney — Bunn-Pher Hill 313-878-9236

Plainwell — The 1882 John Crispe House 616-685-1293

Plymouth — Auburn on Sheldon B&B Inn 313-459-3022

Port Sanilac — Holland's Little House in the Country 810-622-9739
Raymond House Inn 810-622-8800

Rapid River (Hiawatha Nat'l. Forest) — The Buckstop Sporting Lodge and B&B 906-446-3360

Rochester Hills — Paint Creek Bed & Breakfast 810-651-6785

Romeo — Hess Manor Bed & Breakfast 810-752-4726

Saginaw — Brockway House Bed & Breakfast 517-792-0746
Heart House Inn 517-753-3145

St. Joseph — **The Chestnut House Bed & Breakfast 616-983-7413**
  Sausage and Potato Breakfast Torta, page 99
South Cliff Inn Bed & Breakfast 616-983-4881
  Plum Goodie Coffee Cake, page 101

St. Louis — **The Yellow Rose Bed & Breakfast 517-681-5296**
  Creamy Delight Yogurt, page 103

Saline — The Homestead Bed & Breakfast 313-429-9625

Saugatuck — Bayside Inn 616-857-4321
Beechwood Manor 616-857-1587
The Four Seasons Inn—Country Resort 616-857-1955
Kemah Guest House 616-857-2919
  Gooey Cinnamon Ring, page 105

CITY	INN/PHONE

Saugatuck
(cont.)

Maplewood Hotel 616-857-1771

The Newnham SunCatcher Inn 616-857-4249
  Toasted Almond Sticky Buns, page 107

The Park House Bed & Breakfast 616-857-4535
  Fresh Salsa, page 109

The Red Dog Bed & Breakfast 800-357-3250

Saugatuck's Victorian Inn 616-857-3325

Twin Gables Country Inn 616-857-4346

Twin Oaks Inn 616-857-1600

Wickwood Country Inn 616-857-1465
  The Wickwood Summer Tart with Red Pepper Pesto, page 111

Sault Ste. Marie The Water Street Inn 906-632-1900

Scottville Eden Hill B&B 616-757-2023

Sebewaing Rummel's Tree Haven 517-883-2450

Shelby Elmhurst B&B 616-861-4846

The Shepherd's Place Bed & Breakfast 616-861-4298

South Haven Carriage House at the Harbor 616-639-2161

Carriage House at the Park 616-639-1776

A Country Place Bed & Breakfast 616-637-5523
  Southwest Casserole, page 113

Elmhurst Farm Inn 616-637-4633

The Last Resort 616-637-8943

Rainbow's End 616-227-3474

Ross House Bed & Breakfast 616-637-2256

Sand Castle Inn 616-639-1110

The Seymour House Bed & Breakfast 616-227-3918
  Popovers, page 115

Victoria Resort B&B 800-473-7376

Yelton Manor Bed & Breakfast 616-637-5220
  Salsa Elaine, page 117

The Yelton Manor Guest House 616-637-5220

Spring Lake **The Royal Pontaluna Inn 616-798-7271**
  Chocolate Chip (Egg-Free) Cookies, page 119

Sturgis Christmere House Inn 616-651-8303

Suttons Bay Century Farm 616-271-2421

Korner Kottage 616-271-2711

Lee Point Inn on West Grand Traverse Bay 616-271-6770

Morning Glory Beach 616-271-6047

Index of
Recipes

Index

For more information about the Michigan Lake to Lake Bed & Breakfast
Association write to:

Michigan Lake to Lake Bed & Breakfast Association
19271 South Lakeside Road
New Buffalo, Michigan 49117

or look for us on the Internet http://www.laketolake.com

If you have enjoyed this book, you'll love other books and guides from Amherst Press. From food festivals and farmers' markets to fine restaurants, Books-To-Go from Amherst Press is your source for regional interest books, recreational destination guides, and fine cookbooks.

Amherst Press
318 North Main Street
PO Box 296
Amherst, Wisconsin 54406